The Strange Case
of the Missouri Monster

Lyle Blackburn

legend
SCAPE

An Original Publication of LegendScape Publishing

Momo: The Strange Case of the Missouri Monster

Copyright © 2019 by Lyle Blackburn

ISBN: 978-0-578-45679-9

Cover art & illustrations by Claudio Bergamin (@claudiobergamin.art)

Photos courtesy of individual photographers as credited

Edited by A. Dale Triplett (@DaleTriplett)

Book design by Lyle Blackburn

For more information about the author, visit:

www.lyleblackburn.com

Follow the author at:

www.facebook.com/lyleblackburn.official

www.twitter.com/BlackburnLyle

www.instagram.com/lyleblackburn

"For those who witnessed them, the events of July and August that terrorized Louisiana, Mo., never will be forgotten."

- Richard Crowe, FATE Magazine (December 1972)

CONTENTS

INTRODUCTION

Hills, cornfields and woods; woods, hills and cornfields; it was a mesmerizing pattern rolling past my window as I drove north along the west bank of the Mississippi River. I've seen plenty of America's Midwest, but this route was especially scenic in its pastoral peacefulness.

It was mid-morning and I was on my way to a small, riverside town called Louisiana, located in Missouri halfway between Arkansas to the south and Iowa to the north. I didn't see any telltale bayous like I was used to in my neighborly stomping ground of Louisiana state, but there was plenty of green hills and hollers spanning the banks of the famous river that essentially connects the two locations. The Mississippi wasn't visible yet as I motored up Highway 79, but I knew it was there just beyond the woods. If I veered right, crashed through some trees and jumped a hill, I would probably be swimming in it like ol' Huckleberry Finn.

Louisiana (the town) is probably not on most people's tourist radar unless you're tuned into the "50 Miles of Art" – which boasts a renowned "corridor of arts and crafts" between Clarkesville and Hannibal, Missouri – or perhaps if you have an affinity for touring stately Victorian mansions of the antebellum era. It's not to say the town isn't interesting and charmingly scenic, because it absolutely is, but it doesn't have the notoriety of nearby Branson, Missouri, for example.

For me, however, the rather confusingly-named town has always been near the top of my destination wish list. That's because it's home to a particularly fascinating monster tale that's intrigued me since I first read about it as a kid. I can still remember cracking open a copy of Elwood Baumann's book, *Monsters of North America* and turning to a section titled "Momo." On the lead-in page was the word MOMO in big, block letters and a drawing of a hairy, ape-like arm reaching for a pumpkin. I didn't know what this signified, but I sure wanted to find out!

In due time my reading brought me up to speed on what was definitely one of the coolest stories I'd ever heard. Baumann was keen on covering monster stories that grabbed headlines and I was right there with him. This was not the droll stuff my parents were soaking up from television or newspapers, this was real news... *monster news!* In this case, a tall, hairy one who caused so much panic among the citizens of Louisiana, Missouri, that it *did* make national headlines.

Momo, short for "Missouri Monster," quickly took its place alongside my other favorite cryptids such as Bigfoot, the Yeti, Loch Ness Monster, and the Boggy Creek Monster. It was, by all accounts, some kind of hairy biped like Bigfoot, yet it seemed rife with a personality all its own. Its hair was long, black, and matted so that when it hung down from its pumpkin-sized head, its eyes were obscured. More than one witness noted that it was carrying something which appeared to be a dead animal, possibly a dog. And it reeked with a horrible odor that hung in the air long after it slipped back into the woods.

The overall description seemed much like the ubiquitous Bigfoot, yet it aligned closely with the alleged Southern types such as the Boggy Creek Monster and the Skunk Ape, beasts who were infinitely more scraggly, frightening, aggressive, and smelly. Much like the Boggy Creek Monster had in Fouke, Arkansas, Momo sightings in the early 1970s stirred up a rousing reaction of fear, fun, disbelief, and a 'let's go monster hunting' attitude which grabbed the attention of not just Missouri, but anyone in the world with an interest in the burgeoning study of cryptozoology or the paranormal.

Way back when I first discovered 'strange but true' monsters in the pages of Scholastic Readers and library books, I never dreamed I could actually visit the places where they were said to roam or swim. The Yeti was in the snowy mountains of the Himalayas, while the monster of Loch Ness dwelled in far-away Scotland. Even Bigfoot's home was in the distant Pacific Northwest. Those were about as far away from Texas as I thought you could get. When I discovered there were similar creatures said to live much closer, such as the one from Boggy Creek in Arkansas, even then I didn't dream I could actually go there. Within the context of the books, these locations seemed shadowy and mysterious, located far off the beaten path of my family's normal travels. The locations, in my young mind, were the equivalent of King Kong's Skull Island, where unknown creatures hid until such time as meddling explorers or adventurous locals got too close. I was neither an explorer nor a local, and what chance would I have to convince my parents we needed to embark on a monster hunt even if it was within driving distance? It was a subject they simply did not entertain.

But alas, as most of you probably know, I have since breached the reality of these mythical Skull Islands as I've travelled around looking into iconic cryptozoology-monster cases as an adult. And here I was, finally en route to visit one of my favorite creatures, Momo. Well, okay, I didn't totally expect to meet Momo on my first visit, but to step foot in the locations where "the creature" – no matter what it truly was – walked all those years ago would be thrilling enough. It would be like walking into the pages of that old dog-eared book I'd long since lost.

As I got closer to Louisiana (the town[i]), the rolling greenery began to give way to a smattering of man-made structures which represented the culture of the riverside settlement. Some appeared to be relics of the once burgeoning riverboat trade that gave birth to industry and farming along this significant stretch of

---

i   I can see it's going to be a rather confusing name to deal with in this book!

the Mississippi River. There were grain silos and shipping containers sitting dormant upon sprawls of white-gravel ground. There were sturdy iron bridges and old metal buildings, many of which were obviously losing the battle to rust. I crossed several railroad tracks which undoubtedly handled countless trains over the years as they transported goods to and from the area. The mighty river itself was now visible on my right. It carved a striking contrast to the declining statues of industry which stood silent upon its banks.

Eventually, the industrial scenery began to give way to quaint, wood-frame structures and newer buildings as I entered the outskirts of the town proper. White picket fences lined some of the smaller homes, while sprawling, well-mowed lawns surrounded larger ones. All of them hinted at the bucolic appeal of this Midwest gem.

As I entered Louisiana's main thoroughfare, the town's true charm came to life as antebellum architecture began to dominate the view. Massive colonial homes and red-bricked business buildings populated the streets which paralleled the river's edge. A few of the structures were abandoned or in the process of repair, but still its appeal could not be dampened. It was something far different than my home in central Texas. As I drove, I envisioned what the town might have looked like when its prosperity swelled in the late 1800s. Its face was weathered, but its spirit was certainly not lost.

I had a list of monster-related locations to visit, of course, but my first stop was a small visitor's area on the edge of the Mississippi. I've crossed back and forth over the river at various points probably a hundred times, but I've rarely been able to stop and admire its breadth from the bank. As I looked out across the expanse of water, it was not hard to understand its significance to early America and to the town of Louisiana itself. I promptly took a few selfies with my smartphone, careful to position the sign which read "Louisiana: Established 1818" in the background.

Next, I headed over to the town's public library for some journalistic research. I introduced myself to the librarians on duty and announced that I was interested in the Momo story. This is always an interesting point in my journeys — to see what kind of reaction I get from the locals — especially those whom I would expect to be scholars of local history, even if it is the monster-kind. Would they welcome me graciously; would they roll their eyes; or would they have me promptly escorted to the city limits for suggesting we revisit a part of their history that perhaps isn't at the top of their pride list?

I wasn't received by trumpets, but nor did they toss me out by the hat. After introducing myself and giving a short explanation of my intentions, one of the librarians offered to show me the room where they kept all their old newspapers. It was apparently not readily available to anyone who strolled in, so I felt fortunate to be privy to the archives. And these were not the microfiche kind, these were actual newsprints.

I promptly followed the librarian down to the lower level where she unlocked a large oak door. It opened with a creak. I stepped inside as she turned on the light to reveal a room packed with well-kept collections of what seemed like every newspaper the county had ever produced. This, I thought, was gold!

After a friendly reminder to be careful with the fragile pages, she left me on my own to dig for the remains of Momo's official record. I carefully sifted through the volumes until I located the year 1972. In short order I found copies of the *Louisiana Press-Journal,* which had been the primary local purveyor of the stories as they unfolded that summer. I had already collected a good amount of articles from other newspapers and publications, but I knew these would be the most welcome addition to my files. I was no more than 20 minutes into my visit and I had already found Momo. Well, sort of.

The story of Momo is one I had intended to cover in my previous book, *Beyond Boggy Creek: In Search of the Southern Sas-*

quatch. The case fit nicely within the subject matter of the book, which explores the history and modern sightings of Sasquatch-like creatures across the southern United States. However, it simply wouldn't fit. Not only did I end up having to limit the geographic scope of the book to the Deep South (approximately 10 states) because there was so much amazing material, but after doing some extensive research into Momo, I felt the story would be better served as a stand-alone book, much like what I did with the Lizard Man of Bishopville, South Carolina.

The Momo case file is one that spans many aspects of strange phenomenon, which makes it all the more interesting. Along with the Bigfoot angle, there was an associated wave of incidents involving bizarre lights in the skies and woods. Disembodied voices and other odd occurrences were also reported, as Momo-like entities appeared not only in the town of Louisiana but at other points along the Mississippi River basin. The more I researched, the more I realized (as usual) there was more to the story than I ever imagined.

Like so many of these regional monster cases, the effect on the town is also interesting. Not only in terms of how the town reacted to the sudden outbreak of sightings at the time, but how the association with Momo has affected it since. Do the citizens consider it an important part of their history or do they brush it aside with embarrassment? I was there to find out.

After photographing the pertinent pages, I bid farewell to the librarians and headed back to the car. It was time to visit some of the locals and drop by some significant spots related to the case. As I drove away from the library, I looked for any residual signs of the monster's old mania. I thought perhaps I might find a "Monster Auto Shop" or a "Momo Deli," or at least something which had incorporated a monster mascot. I saw plenty of businesses, but none with even a hint of the monster's memory.

I spent the next few hours meeting with a few locals and snapping photos of whatever I thought might be significant before zig-zagging my way back through town and turning onto historic Georgia Street, which serves as the main thoroughfare from the river's edge to the southwest edge of town. As I drove along admiring a variety of older, colonial homes, I caught sight of a tree-covered hill that loomed behind them to my right. I knew instantly it had to be Marzolf Hill.

The hill is perhaps mundane to those who live in the quaint houses below it, but it's nonetheless significant in terms of the town's infamous monster. It's where the most famous sighting occurred and where hunters once plunged into its thick underbrush in all seriousness to flush out a thing which had beset the town with uneasy excitement.

In the context of daylight and quaint neighborhoods, it didn't look as ominous as one might imagine. Yet still, seeing it in person took me back to the first time I'd read about it in Baumann's old book. To me, it still represented a miniature, modern Skull Island; one that had risen up in the very heartland of America.

I took a quick right at the next street and drove towards it. As I neared the base, Marzolf Hill's reputation seemed to cast a palpable shadow separate from those of the midday sun. I don't know if this shadow was apparent to others driving nearby, but I sensed it just the same. Whatever secrets the hill holds may never be known, but I was there to see it for myself. Momo is a case I've been wanting to explore for a long time, and now was my opportunity to investigate, celebrate, and sort out a mystery that has become one of the most notable in terms of American cryptozoology.

I made one last turn and headed straight towards the heart of its mystery. In due time I would be standing in the same spot the alleged Missouri Monster had been standing all those years ago. Here, my friends, is the true story.

Chapter 1.

IT CAME FROM THE WOODS

Something watched from the shadows as Joan Mills and Mary Ryan prepared to picnic at the edge of a wooded thicket. As they made sandwiches, they didn't notice whatever lurked in the trees. Their focus was elsewhere at the moment, anticipating lunch and a leisurely respite from driving.

It was the summer of 1971 and the two women had been traveling in their Volkswagen south on Highway 79 bound for St. Louis, Missouri. At around noon they decided to veer off on a small scenic turnout in Pike County so they could eat while enjoying the picturesque scenery. The spot where they stopped was just north of Louisiana, Missouri, where the Mississippi River carves a winding border along the eastern edge of the state. The region is dotted with cornfields and vast, forested hills which spread for miles along the famous waterway. By all accounts, it would have been the perfect spot for a picnic… that is, until something unexpected and altogether frightening emerged from the woods.

As Joan and Mary were eating they began to smell a rank, revolting odor. Joan suggested the smell was coming from a family of skunks, but it just didn't seem like the usual smell of a skunk, or even a whole family of them. As they were recoiling from the stench, Joan saw something walk from the brushy thicket a short distance away. She pointed in horror as Mary turned to look.

"I turned around and this thing was standing there in the

thicket," Joan Mills would later report.[1] "The weeds were pretty high and I just saw the top part of this creature. It was staring down at us."

The creature was tall and primate-like. As it began to approach the women, it made a strange gurgling noise.

"It had hair [all] over the body as if it was an ape," Mary recalled. "Yet, the face was definitely human. It was more like a hairy human." The apish abomination walked upright on two feet with its arms dangling low to its knees. "The arms were partially covered with hair, but the hands and the palms were hairless," she added. "We had plenty of time to see this."

The terrified women jumped to their feet and ran toward the car. When they reached it they jumped inside and locked the door. Joan frantically looked for the keys but it was no use. In her haste, she had left her purse sitting on the weathered picnic table where the creature now stood. The car keys were inside the purse.

The thing began to walk towards the car as the women watched in fear. When it reached the vehicle, it placed its hands on the hood then came around to the door. The women were absolutely frantic.

"Finally, my arm hit the horn ring and the thing jumped straight in the air and moved back," Mills explained. She continued to beep the horn, forcing the creature to retreat. It seemed alarmed at first, but eventually realized the horn wasn't dangerous. The women watched as it returned to the picnic table and sniffed around their lunch. After a few moments, it scooped up one of the abandoned sandwiches and devoured it in one bite. It then picked up the purse, inspected it briefly, and tossed it aside before finally returning to the woodline where it disappeared into the brush.

Joan waited a few moments before deciding it was safe enough to jump out of the car and grab her purse. Once she got the car started, the women sped down the small road and screeched back onto the highway. Whatever it was that lurked in those woods, they never wanted to see it again.

Mills and Ryan passed through the small town of Louisiana and kept driving south on Highway 79 until they eventually reached St. Louis. Once there, they immediately contacted the Missouri State Highway Patrol and filed an official report. They knew no one was likely to believe their story, but they felt it was important to report it. Even though they managed to escape unharmed, perhaps the next travelers wouldn't be so lucky.

"We'd have difficulty proving that the experience occurred," Mills wrote, "but all you have to do is go into those hills to realize that an army of those things could live there undetected."

At that moment, she had no way of knowing Missouri was on the cusp of one of the strangest and most notable monster cases to ever creep out of the American backwoods.

Incidents at Marzolf Hill

When Mills and Ryan reported their bizarre encounter in July 1971, by all accounts, it was an isolated incident. The state police, who were undoubtedly skeptical, had received no other reports of an ape in the area, human-like or otherwise. And since no actual crime had taken place (save for sandwich theft), the officers simply wrote it off as a silly prank and shooed the women out the door.

There was nothing else Mills and Ryan could do since there was no way to corroborate their story. That is, until one year later when a series of similarly bizarre incidents began to command news headlines. Apparently, something was loose in the Missouri countryside, and it was about to gain nationwide attention!

On the afternoon of July 11, 1972, eight-year-old Terry Harrison and his five-year-old brother, Walley, were playing behind their house in Louisiana, Missouri, when they heard a low, throaty growl. Moments later, Terry looked up to see a huge, hulking figure standing approximately 15 feet away. Their home was located at the end of Allen Street, a dead-end road at the foot of a heavily wooded area known as Marzolf Hill. It was not out of the ordinary to see a wild animal there, but this was no ordinary animal. It was tall and stood upright like a human, yet was covered in long, black hair which obscured its face. It had no neck and a large, pumpkin-sized head, and reeked with a terrible odor that wafted into the air. To makes things worse, the thing had splatters of red on its fur, like blood, and held what appeared to be a lifeless dog in one arm.

Terry panicked and ran toward the house screaming. Walley followed close behind. Their sister Doris, who was fifteen at the time, was cleaning the sink in the bathroom. When her brothers came into the house hollering, she looked out the window and saw the creature standing near the hill. She watched for a few horrified moments until it turned and ran into the woods.

"It was... six or seven feet tall, black and hairy," Doris told reporters at the time. "It stood like a man, but it didn't look like one."[2]

Horrified, Doris told her brothers to stay inside while she called their mother at work. She locked the door and prayed the beast would not return and try to force its way in.

When Betty Harrison received the panicked call from her daughter, she immediately called her husband, Edgar – who was also working – and told him to get home fast. Something weird was going on and she was worried about the kids.

Within 30 minutes Edgar Harrison arrived home. He first calmed the children and then searched the area behind the home. He found no trace of the creature itself, but did find an area of flattened brush just 50 feet from the house where the thing had apparently been standing. He also found what he believed to be "faint footprints in the dust with black hairs around them."[3]

Once he was satisfied the creature – or whatever it might have been – was no longer there, he asked his son Terry for further details. "It was big and it was weaving back and forth," Harrison said of his son's description. "It had long black hair hanging down all over. He could not see its face."[4]

Terry told his father "the dog had red stuff on it," which he assumed was blood. Edgar looked, but found no traces of blood in the "stamped down circle" where the thing had been standing. Terry seemed a bit uncertain whether it was actually a dog the thing was holding. He could only say that it looked like it had four legs and was covered in black hair just like the creature. Edgar wondered if it was, in actuality, one of its offspring. It was even more alarming to think there might be a group of these things living on the hill.

The incident was thoroughly frightening for the family, and it was just the beginning. Shortly after the incident, one of their dogs became violently ill and vomited for hours. Later that night, around 1:30 a.m., Edgar heard noises which sounded like a prowler behind the home. He could hear the "popping of brush, as if something were running through the woods."[5] Edgar enlisted the help of four neighbors who assisted in searching the area of Marzolf Hill, but nothing was found. The following night came with much of the same. Noises and searches, but this time with eight men joining Harrison in the hunt.

On Friday July 14 the intensity increased. That night the Harrison family was hosting a weekly prayer meeting at their home with approximately 30 attendees from the local Pentecostal Church. At roughly 9:00 p.m., after most of the parishioners had left, Edgar Harrison was standing outside with the 12 remaining guests when they saw several "balls of light" move from east to west, just over the trees in the neighboring yard. They saw two others – one white and one green – go down in the vicinity of a nearby school. No one could figure out what kind of lights they were.

A short time later, after everyone had left, Harrison was relaxing outside playing guitar when he heard a strange sound. "I heard something that sounded like a loud growl," he told reporters. "It got louder and louder and kept coming closer."[6] His family heard it too and came running out of the house. They jumped into the car and pleaded with Edgar to get in and drive them to safety. Edgar wanted to stay and see what was making the noise, but his wife and kids would have none of it, so he reluctantly got in the car and drove off.

As they were proceeding away from the home, the Harrisons were confronted by an almost surreal sight. "Over 40 people were coming toward my house, some of them carrying guns," he said. "They had heard the same noise we did."[7] They had also seen the unexplained balls of light. Edgar stopped the car, but before he could converse with the crowd, Mrs. Harrison screamed out of the car window: 'here it comes!' The crowd quickly turned and fled down the street in a panic.

Both Edgar Harrison and a woman named Maxine Minor called the local police to report the strange sights and sounds. Chief Shelby Ward fielded both calls and decided to dispatch two officers to the scene. Officers John Whitaker and Jerry Floyd went to the Harrison home and searched the vicinity, but neither of them saw or heard anything.

After the police left, Harrison and several neighbors set out to search Marzolf Hill more thoroughly. As they were scanning the woods with flashlights, they found a dilapidated old building. The interior reeked with a pungent odor which Harrison described as a "moldy, horse smell or garbage smell."[8] It seemed like a probable hiding place, yet they saw no signs of the suspected creature.

Moving on, the group continued to explore as much as they could of the ominous hill for the next few hours. It was a daunting task, however. The trees and undergrowth were thick, and in the darkness anything could have easily hid just beyond the scope of their feeble flashlight beams. Finally, they gave up and returned home empty-handed.

The next day dawned with an eerie silence, but that didn't do much to calm the nerves of Edgar Harrison. With a monstrous, dog-killing beast on the loose and a gang of armed vigilantes chasing it, he feared for his family's safety. When they awoke, he had them pack enough belongings to last them for the immediate future and headed off for town where the family owned a restaurant. The Harrisons would sleep there until either the incident blew over or the beast was apprehended.

Fearful Frenzy

By now it wasn't only the Harrisons on edge. The entire town of Louisiana was in the clutches of a fearful frenzy. As details of the Marzolf Hill incidents began to make news headlines, other reports began to surface. First, Mrs. Clarence Lee, who lived a block and a half away, said she heard a terrible, growling, animal sound the same afternoon the Harrison kids had seen the hairy thing. She told reporters it was "carrying on something terrible."[9] Robert Parsons and his wife also heard the sound. A nearby farmer confirmed that a dog he'd given to his daughter had been missing for at least a week. He wondered if it was the dog the beast had been clutching in its bloody hands.

Another town resident, Pat Howard, saw a dark, man-like figure walk across a road near the hill at approximately 5:00 a.m. on the night Harrison and the others were searching.[10] It could not be identified.

A few days later, on July 18, two boys were hiking on Marzolf Hill when they came upon "the thing standing in the woods."[11] When it growled, they bolted in terror and reported the sighting to police. They said it had a foul stench and resembled a bear. Around the same time, a woman told reporters at Channel 7 she had definitely seen a "black, long-haired thing" cross the highway into Louisiana.[12] Yet another resident told Chief Ward he saw the thing near Highway 79 and it appeared to be carrying a sheep or dog in its mouth. Still others claimed to have also smelled a terrible odor while walking near the hill. One of these was a Mr. Houchins who said he caught a whiff of a strange scent while something was "thrashing about on Marzolf Hill."[13]

Chief Ward was skeptical of the reports, but there was no denying he had a problem on his hands. If it were a bear or even a prankster, somebody was likely to get hurt, especially with the growing number of citizens who had taken up arms and plunged into the woods looking for anything tall, dark and hairy.

"There is something out there and it has the people of this town scared to death," Ward stated at the time.[14] "I get about 10 calls a night about it from good, reliable citizens. I've been trying to convince people it's probably a bear or a practical joker in a gorilla costume, but I'll have to admit it could be something else. The more I keep hearing about it from people, the more difficult it is for me to be skeptical."

Given the situation, Ward decided to organize an official search. On the morning of July 19, Ward assembled a group of 20 men which included eight police officers, State Conservation Of-

The woods of Marzolf Hill
(Photo by Lyle Blackburn)

ficer Gus Artus, Edgar Harrison, four out-of-state reporters, and some local volunteers. Gus Artus was placed in charge of the operation, which was intended to either find evidence of the 'monster' or put the town at ease. "We want to be able to say that we have made a complete search," Artus told the group as they assembled.[15]

Once they were ready, the search party headed to Marzolf Hill where they combed the woods for nearly three hours. In the process, the men spread out about 30 feet apart and checked as much of the brush as they could, scanning for anything: whether it be footprints, hair, or even the remains of dead dogs. During the search, they came upon several landowners who were either in favor of the effort — or completely resistant to the idea. One particularly disagreeable landowner called them 'crazy' and ordered them to get off his land. The searchers did the best they could, but in the end, whatever it was – be it person or animal – apparently laid low and the search ended in failure.

Maxine Minor, who had called the police several days earlier, felt the search was unsuccessful because it had been conducted during the day rather than at night. She told Ward she had heard "the creature growl on several occasions" but it was always after dark between 10:00 p.m. and 10:30 p.m. The vocalization, she said, started as a "low growl" and ended as a "high-pitched scream."[16]

Later that day, Harrison and nearly 40 other people "heard an animal growling and roaring near George Minor's house on Dougherty-Pike [Road]."[17] Minor's son, Lynn, theorized it might have been a "hog gone wild, or a wildcat" or even a "prank," but he wasn't sure. The only thing he and the others could agree on was that something bizarre was happening, and Marzolf Hill was becoming dangerous due to the growing number of people there with firearms.

On July 20, Richard Crowe, a reporter for both *The Irish Times* newspaper in Chicago and *FATE* magazine, arrived on the scene with Loren Smith, an attorney from Skokie, Illinois. According to Crowe in his subsequent FATE magazine article, they first reported to the police station and were then escorted to the Harrison residence. When they arrived at about 9:30 p.m., they found Edgar, Doris, and her boyfriend Richard Bliss "camped out waiting for something to happen."[18] The Harrison family was still staying at their restaurant in town, but Edgar, and occasionally others, kept a nightly vigil at their house on Allen Street hoping the creature would return. Mr. Harrison seemed intent on solving whatever mystery had befallen his family.

After Edgar brought Crowe and Smith up to date on the

Searchers on Marzolf Hill - July 19, 1972
(Credit: Louisiana Press-Journal)

latest happenings, he showed them the spot where his kids had seen the creature standing. "There was a circular spot in the brush where leaves and twigs had been stripped from the branches," Crowe noted.[19]

Next, Harrison and Richard Bliss led them up a path behind the house onto Marzolf Hill. Within a short distance they came to the remains of an old garbage dump, which looked to have been recently disturbed. They could see tin cans and bottles which had been dug up and strewn about. Nearby, Harrison pointed out a spot where the graves of two dogs had also been dug up, their bones scattered.

As they progressed, the hill became steeper and landscape wilder with dense trees and tangled brush. Eventually, the men came upon what appeared to be two impressions in the ground. The first was over ten inches long and five inches wide and resembled a "large human footprint."[20] The other was "five inches long and curved," like the print of a hand. Given the dry, hard soil surface, Crowe estimated "it would take a minimum of 200 pounds of pressure to create such impressions."

Harrison then showed Crowe and Smith the abandoned shack where he and the group of previous searchers had smelled the terrible odor. There was a pile of leaves and debris in the corner, which they theorized might be some sort of sleeping nest. While they were examining the building, Harrison's dog, who had been tagging along, suddenly ran off. Crowe said in that instant they smelled "an overwhelming stench that could only be described as resembling rotten flesh or foul, stagnant water."[21]

Shortly thereafter, they heard several dogs begin to bark furiously in the direction of Dougherty-Pike Road, a short distance away. Harrison was sure the monster was responsible. The men readied their cameras and scanned the woods with their flashlights, but nothing emerged. After five minutes, the odor was gone and all went silent. The men returned to the house where they kept vigil until 3:00 a.m. Twice more they smelled the repulsive odor, but never saw anything.

The creature's shadowy nature was underscored by the continuing reports. A few days later, another local named Ellis Minor came forward to recount his own chilling encounter with the beast. Minor, whom a reporter described as a 63-year-old "grizzled, toothless fisherman," had been living along the Mississippi since he was six-years-old and knew everything that walked, slithered, or swam in the region. Or so he thought.[22]

Minor said that around 10:30 p.m. on July 21 he was sitting in front of his house on River Road when his bird dog began to growl. The dog rarely growled at anything, so Minor flipped on his flashlight and aimed it in the direction the dog was looking. "I shone a light, right there about 20 feet up the road," he explained. "It was standing there, hair black as coal. I couldn't see its eyes or face – it had hair nearly down to its chest." The thing was at least six feet tall with hair that covered its entire body. It stood upright

Railroad crossing at River Road on the edge of the Mississippi
(Photo by Lyle Blackburn)

on two legs in the center of the road. "As soon as I threw the light on it, it whirled and took off. It's the first time I ever seen an ugly looking thing like that."[23]

Minor noted that if his dog hadn't growled, the thing might have crept right through his yard. It seemed to be headed for the river which runs parallel to River Road, only a short distance from Minor's home. When the light hit it, the figure turned and ran across the adjacent railroad track and disappeared in the dark woods beyond. When asked what he would have done if the thing would've walked into his yard, Minor professed: "I don't know which would've run faster – me or the dog."

Minor might have been missing a few teeth, but he was respected around town. Patrolman John Whitaker, who had responded to one of the Harrison incidents, told the media: "I've known Ellis Minor all my life and I've never known him to make anything up. Something just might be up in these hills."

Timmy McCormick, a young teen, said he also saw it in the woods. He described it as looking "just the way Mr. [Edgar] Harrison said."[24] His mother wouldn't let him report it to the police for fear people would think he was crazy. But apparently it was okay to speak with a journalist. "Maybe I am [crazy]," McCormick quipped, "but I wouldn't go into those woods again for anything."

Things got even weirder on the night of July 29 while Edgar Harrison and several local college students were exploring Marzolf Hill. They were standing near the top of the hill when they heard what sounded like a gunshot from the road below. They immediately rushed down to investigate. When they got close to the road, "they all distinctly heard an old man's voice saying, 'You boys stay out of these woods.'"[25] The chilling voice seemed to have come from a nearby cluster of trees "no more than 20 feet wide by 50 feet." They searched the entire area thoroughly, but found nothing. They were stunned.

A few days later, a farmer named Freddie Robbins found a set of mysterious footprints on his farm eight miles south of town. They were roughly oval shaped and appeared to have three long, thin toes. On August 3, more strange footprints turned up at the rural home of Mr. and Mrs. Bill Suddarth, who lived northwest of town on Dougherty-Pike Road. According to Richard Crowe in his *FATE* magazine article, that morning just as light was creeping over the horizon, Mrs. Suddarth noticed her dogs were acting nervously. A few moments later, she heard a "high-pitched howl" very close to the house. Alarmed, Mr. Suddarth grabbed a flashlight and went outside to investigate. He didn't see whatever made the sound, but in looking around the exterior of the home he found four large, three-toed tracks in the muddy soil of their garden. They were unlike any kind of animal track Suddarth had ever seen.

Concerned, Suddarth phoned his friend Clyde Penrod and asked him to come over and take a look. Penrod had seen the tracks at the Robbins' farm, so he was interested in what Suddarth had found. Penrod grabbed some plaster casting material and headed over.

When Penrod arrived, he examined the mysterious tracks and the circumstances in which they were left. He was completely puzzled. "It was 20 to 25 feet from the tracks to anything else," he told Crowe. "I can't understand how they were made." There were no other tracks, either leading to or away from the garden. Even if they had been left by a person, it would have been impossible to get to the garden without leaving some kind of tracks. It had rained much of the previous night, so there was plenty of muddy soil surrounding the Suddarth's house. Penrod proceeded to make a copy of the best track using the plaster. He felt that no matter what it was, it needed to be preserved.

On the afternoon of August 4, four boys – including two of Edgar Harrison's sons – were fishing north of town at the Salt River when they saw what appeared to be a large, dark animal swimming across the water. According to the *Louisiana Press-Jour-*

The track cast by Clyde Penrod
(Courtesy of Christina Windmiller)

nal, Ernest Shade (16), Rossie Shade (7), Lewis Harrison (13), and Fred Harrison (10) were quietly fishing for perch and catfish around 4:00 p.m. when Ernest noticed a dark object in the river.[26] He didn't pay much attention at first, but when he realized it was moving, he and the other boys began to watch.

"The object was moving in a definite line against the current, up-stream," Fred told a reporter at the time. It appeared to be an animal with a head "bigger than a human" and shoulders which were "sticking out of the water." The boys thought it might be a bear, but they weren't close enough to say for sure.

"We looked at it until it got out of sight and then we left," said Lewis. With reports of a monster on the loose – including the dramatic sighting by Lewis' own siblings – the boys didn't want to hang around and risk finding out just what the thing really was.

Whether there was a real-life monster or not, authorities were continually dealing with the problems it caused. When someone reported a sighting at a private landing field close to Louisiana and also at nearby Haerr Field, the Federal Aviation Agency (FAA) instructed airport officials and pilots to be on the lookout for the creature or any "unidentified object."[27] Back in town, Chief Ward was still dealing with the increasing number of townsfolk and outsiders who were hellbent on hunting the thing down. To top it off, reporters began circling the area like vultures with notepads. Their headlines would only make it worse.

Hairy Headlines

It didn't take long for the events to create a certified sensation, not only locally but well beyond. Stories were initially covered by the town's *Louisiana Press-Journal* newspaper, and within a short time by a wider range of papers such as the *St. Louis Post-Dispatch*, *St. Louis Globe-Democrat*, *Kansas City Times* (MO), *Bowling Green Times* (MO), *Centralia Sentinel* (IL), *Decatur Review* (IL), *Pittsburg Post-Gazette* (PA), *Patriot-News* (PA), *La Trobe Bulletin* (PA), and *Nevada State Journal*, among others. When the articles were picked by the United Press International (UPI) wire, they found an even larger audience in the *Chicago Tribune*, *New York Times*, *National Enquirer*, and of all things, the *Wall Street Journal*.

When the reports first hit newsprint, the monster was called by several names including the Pike County Monster, Mystery Beast, Hairy Biped, and The Thing. But it was Momo, a clever play on "Missouri Monster" that caught on as the endearing favorite and the one which endures today. The name was short, catchy, and gave the creature an almost cuddly vibe, despite its reputation as a foul-smelling, pumpkin-headed, hairy beast with a penchant for carrying dead animals.

As the story of Momo spread, it attracted more and more curious travelers, reporters, and monster hunters who descended on the little town of Louisiana in droves. A dozen Navy men from Texas were among them, as well as carloads of people from surrounding states such as Illinois. The hotels and restaurants became filled with visitors.

The weird wave of tourism was a shock for townsfolk at first, but they quickly adapted. The restaurants added "Giant Monster-Burger" specials to their menus while retail stores advertised "Momo-Sized Bargains." Nearly every advertisement in *The Louisiana Press-Journal* began to incorporate some form of monster motif, whether it was the wording, an accompanying drawing of Momo, or both. Even larger advertisers, such as the JC Penneys and Gibson's chain stores, got in on the act with "Monster Sales" and monstrous beasts in their ads. Given that Momo was essentially a rank, dead-dog toting thing of unknown origin, it was really quite ironic, especially in the cases where Momo was used to advertise food products.

The story of Momo gained so much attention even the *Wall Street Journal* was curious... not about the monster per se,

Newspaper coverage
(Credit: Louisiana Press-Journal)

but about the economics of the whole affair. In a phone call to Louisiana's town clerk, Jeanne Hallows, one of their New York reporters asked "how the monster had affected Louisiana's business?"[28] She confirmed it had definitely helped the town's business, and helped to put Louisiana "on the map" for tourists.

Momo was undoubtedly a boon for the town with the additional influx of revenue. The monster hunters, however, were more than a simple tourism problem for Chief Shelby Ward and his police force. They were an absolute menace. A group of at least 20 men showed up at a local hotel restaurant after reading the news headlines. While eating breakfast, they asked the waitress 'where Star Hill was' and said they were going to 'hunt the monster.'[ii] Luckily one of Chief Ward's officers caught wind of their intentions and ordered them to leave town before they could plunge into the woods.[29]

Not all of the would-be monster seekers could be sent off so easily, however. Dozens of armed men were already swarming Marzolf Hill and the surrounding woods ready to shoot anything which looked remotely big and hairy. In the process they trespassed on private property, trampled crops, and broke down fences. Shots rang out from the woods at all hours, and residents could only wonder if they'd shot the creature, somebody's livestock, or worse, some*body*. On one occasion, two hunters mistook a bull for the monster and shot it dead. The owner was furious and called police, but there was little that Chief Ward could do, since there was no way of knowing which of the errant monster hunters was responsible.[30]

Ward was concerned the next victim might be human or that some of the vigilantes would get lost in the deep woods surrounding his small town. The woods were filled with plenty of known hazards such as venomous snakes and thick briars. The

---

ii   Marzolf Hill was also known as "Star Hill" due to a lighted Christmas star placed there annually.

Monster ads circa July-August 1972
(Credit: Louisiana Press-Journal)

hills were also dotted with caves and cliffs just waiting for amateur sleuths to make one wrong step. The potential for human disaster was much more worrisome than the monster itself in the eyes of law enforcement. Not to mention the time officers were spending on the phone listening to various reports and complaints. For Ward and his deputies, it was one big hairy headache.

In an effort to prevent accidental shootings, Chief Ward declared Marzolf Hill "off limits." A wooden roadblock was placed across one of the main dirt roads leading from Kentucky Street to the top of the hill, while other deterrents were placed accordingly. Local resident, Nelson Clark, told reporters from *The Louisiana Press-Journal* at the time: "Something had to be done. There were people all up and down the hill, carrying rifles, shotguns and pistols."[31]

The news coverage also attracted investigators of the paranormal kind who specialized in tracking hairy bipeds and extraterrestrial beings. Two of these were Hayden C. Hewes and Daniel Garcia of the International Unidentified Flying Object Bureau. The duo came from Oklahoma City to investigate the incidents under the presumption that the creature may be an extraterrestrial visitor. Bigfoot type creatures were occasionally associated with UFO activity, and since witnesses had reported seeing strange lights in the sky, Hewes and Garcia felt it was a possibility.[32]

Upon their arrival, the two investigators looked for tracks supposedly found behind an auto service station on Georgia Street. Next, they headed to the Harrison home where they interviewed Edgar Harrison and Richard Bliss, and looked around the property. The police gave them permission to camp on Marzolf Hill that night, provided they submit an official report of any activity or findings. The night, however, was quiet.

The next day, Hewes and Garcia were interviewed by a United Press International reporter and were filmed at the Harrison residence by a television crew out of Columbia, Missouri. During the interview, Hewes described the creature as being an upright, hairy biped with a "large pumpkin-shaped head and glowing orange eyes." He said the alleged creature "could be connected with creatures from outer space," but admitted that on the other hand, "it might turn out to be nothing."[33]

The resulting press coverage with mentions of UFOs and animals from outer space brought an even weirder angle to the case. Subsequent articles tended to echo Hewes' description of "glowing orange eyes," although as reporter Richard Crowe pointed out, this was not entirely accurate. "The best witnesses clearly stated the eyes were indistinguishable in the long hair," Crowe said.

While some connected Momo with Bigfoot, others, like Hewes, sided with the extraterrestrial angle. Still others believed it was all hogwash and hoaxes. But no matter what the explanation was, there was little doubt something strange was going on in

Missouri. Something that, perhaps, had been going on for longer than anyone realized.

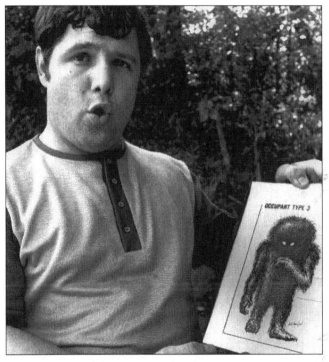

Hayden Hewes displays an illustration by Hal Crawford which he felt matched descriptions of the creature (Credit: United Press International)

Chapter 2.

BEASTS ON THE LOOSE

The more Momo was publicized and investigated, the more it became apparent something big and hairy may have been stalking the region for a much longer period of time. The heavy news coverage prompted other witnesses to come forward with reports which, prior to then, would've seemed irrelevant or perhaps crazy. Subsequent investigations by police and paranormal aficionados brought out even more. As these were tied together, a monstrous case began to build like steam on the mighty Mississip'.

One of the most significant tie-ins was the harrowing experience reported by Joan Mills and Mary Ryan one year earlier. The spot where they were confronted by the creepy, ape-like figure was only two miles from Marzolf Hill. At the time the women reported the event to the State Police, they could have never predicted an outbreak of similar sightings would erupt in the small town one year later.

Harrison himself noted that since the Momo reports had been publicized, a family in the area told him their son had seen a "big, tall, black ugly thing" in the vicinity of a nearby abandoned school building in July of 1971.[34] This is interesting since there's no way this witness could have known about Mills' and Ryan's corresponding encounter that same month since theirs wasn't yet publicized.

According to John Green, a preeminent journalist and author who collected Bigfoot reports, in the summer of 1970 a sighting of an "unknown creature" was allegedly reported to the Pike County Sheriff's Department.[35] While the description is vague and the witness referred to as an "unnamed informant," the coincidence cannot be overlooked.

An even more timely sighting occurred on June 30, less than two weeks before the Harrison incident. The report was documented by John Schuessler, an aerospace engineer and assistant director of the Midwest UFO Network (now known as the Mutual UFO Network), who had also become interested in the case. Two men – identified as Tim and V.M. – told Schuessler they were fishing that evening along the Cuivre River south of Louisiana (Missouri) when they looked up to see "someone, or something, wading into the middle of the river" about 250 feet upstream. "The someone was big and hairy."[36]

At first they thought it was a "hippie" (a person who wore long hair at the time) since they could only see its shoulders and head above the water. But as they watched, they began to realize it was not a person. It appeared to be "a large creature walking armpit-to-armpit across the river." They estimated the water was around 5.5 feet deep at that point, so the thing was rather tall and it "waded with ease, appearing to be extremely strong by the way it crossed."

When the thing emerged from the river and walked onto the bank, Tim retreated up the embankment, fearing the thing would come in their direction. V.M. stayed where he was for the moment, apparently unseen by the creature as it began walking along the riverbank towards them. When the thing got within 150 feet, V.M. also panicked and ran up the hillside to join Tim. When they looked back, the creature was scrambling up the hillside further down the river, as if it had been startled by the commotion.

The two frightened fisherman eventually located a ranger from the nearby Cuivre River State Park and told him what they'd seen. The ranger was skeptical, however, it wasn't the first weird incident of the evening. Not long before, another couple was fishing upstream from the location when they heard "grunts and groans" as if someone or some*thing* was in pain.[37] They were so unnerved by the sounds, they stopped fishing and ran for safety. They too found the ranger and reported the incident.

The ranger agreed to accompany Tim and V.M. back to the location to recover their fishing gear, which they'd left in their haste. When they arrived, they found no sign of the mysterious "animal" but did find what appeared to be a large, three-toed footprint in the mud where the thing had emerged from the water. At the time, nobody was sure what to make of it. Only later did investigators connect that three-toed track with those found near Louisiana. The Cuivre River is 30 miles south of Louisiana, but is essentially connected by a rolling landscape of heavy woods and cornfields which runs along the west bank of the Mississippi River. Not a very long distance considering the potential range of a large animal.

Cuivre River
(Photo by Lyle Blackburn)

Walter Andrus, another MUFON director who investigated the Momo case, felt it was "definitely not a hoax generated by children." Like Hewes and Crowe, he interviewed Edgar Harrison and was shown a drawing of the creature young Doris had seen behind their house. The sketch, in Andrus' opinion, looked very much like the animal the fishermen described at the Cuivre River.

A similar water-related sighting was reported to John Schuessler after he was interviewed on a St. Louis television station regarding the Momo events. A woman told Schuessler her husband was fishing near Foley, Missouri, "when he was terrified by a large shaggy creature which came up out of the water." The woman said she and the rest of the family had "been teasing him about it," but after hearing the Momo reports they were not so sure. Foley is also located 30 miles south of Louisiana, just east of the Cuivre River.

Twenty miles south of that location, two teenage girls claimed to have seen a "bear-like creature" walking upright near a wooded area outside the town of O'Fallon on July 24 around sunset.[38] A short distance away in New Haven, a girl claimed to have seen a gray-colored, hairy creature walking upright in a field during the early morning hours just four days earlier.[39]

Another spooky incident which came to light because of the headlines involved the dairy farmer, Mr. Wendorff, whose bull had been shot by monster hunters outside the town of Louisiana. Wendorff said that just prior to the Harrison's sighting, he was awakened one morning when his dogs began to bark furiously.[40] The dogs always slept outside on the porch and were rarely roused by anything, especially at that hour. It was around 5:00 a.m., close to the time Wendorff got up anyway, so he quickly dressed and went to see what the trouble was.

As soon as the farmer opened the kitchen door, the dogs were at his feet cowering as though they were scared. It was very unusual for his dogs to be frightened, so Wendorff stepped outside to have a look around. He immediately felt an eerie silence and smelled an odor that reminded him of "firecrackers." It was strange unto itself, but that wasn't the only odd thing.

As Wendorff scanned the area in the hazy morning light, he caught sight of a dark, humanoid figure "heading across a field in the direction of the river." It walked with "an odd, shuffling gait" and looked something like "a very large old man wearing a fur overcoat."

A bit unnerved and concerned that someone would trespass on his land, the farmer hurried inside to grab his rifle. He figured if he shot a couple of rounds into the air, it would send an adequate warning. As he fumbled in a drawer for some rounds, his wife asked what was going on. Wendorff simply replied: "There's something out there."

When he returned to the porch and looked out across the field, however, he could no longer see the strange figure. Whatever it was had disappeared from sight. He set his rifle on the porch, keeping it close by just in case. The fact that his dogs had cowered still had him rattled.

Later, after the sun was overhead, Wendorff took a more thorough look around his property. He inspected the areas around his outlying farm buildings but found nothing disturbed. Afterwards, he drove down to the river in the direction the figure had been heading and got out to look around. There he found a strange set of tracks leading down to the water. They looked animal-like, but he couldn't tell what kind of animal had made them.

With no explanation and no pressing reason to tell anyone outside of his wife, Wendorff put the incident out of his mind. Later, when others in the area began to report sightings of a large, hairy creature, he realized it could have been the same thing he'd seen. He then went on record describing it as "something part way between a great big man in a fur overcoat, a bear walking on its hind legs, and a sort of gorilla-like thing."

Mississippi River bank just outside the town of Louisiana
(Photo by Lyle Blackburn)

Close Calls

Not all of the Pike County sightings were made public at the time. As with many of these monster cases, some individuals who had encounters didn't want to come forward at the risk of sounding crazy, or simply didn't want to get involved in the media circus. One such person was Bill Riley, a man who lived in the nearby town of Hannibal, Missouri. According to Riley, he was chased by some kind of humanoid beast on July 15, a mere four days after Momo was sighted at the Harrison home.

In 2001, Riley told a reporter from the *St. Louis Post-Dispatch* that it was around eight-feet-tall and gave off a horrible stench. "A lot of people don't want to admit publicly what they saw, out of fear of being the butt of humor," he explained.[41] So he kept the incident to himself for years until he finally confided in his future wife.

Riley later submitted his report to the Bigfoot Field Research Organization (BFRO) after he came upon their website while researching other Bigfoot sightings in the area. According to Riley, he and a friend set out for a party that was supposed to be happening on the evening of July 15, 1972, in the rural area of Pike County. However, the party was a bust so they ended up leaving. "When we got to the place out of town," Riley said, "I took off by myself down the road towards the east back to Route 70."[42] After walking for approximately 30 minutes, the wind shifted and he got a whiff of a strong odor which smelled like a "cross between a skunk and rotten flesh." As he continued to walk he became aware that someone was walking approximately 300 feet away in the trees beside the road. He was close to a pasture, so he figured it must have been a farmer rounding up his cows.

"I thought it was kind of late for a farmer to be bringing his cows in as they were in a big hurry to get away from him," Riley explained. "About that time I heard a God-awful blood curdling scream which I thought was the cattle screaming."

Riley stopped walking and looked at what he believed was the farmer standing in the trees. The farmer had stopped walking as well and appeared to be looking back at Riley. Confused and somewhat spooked, Riley started walking again, this time a bit faster. The farmer too started walking again, matching pace with Riley. By now Riley was nearly running.

"As I continued east… he matched my every move and would stop and stare when I did," Riley continued. "The cows were gone by now and the stench was getting stronger as, what I thought was a man, angled his way closer to me."

Riley stopped again and looked closer. Now he could see that it wasn't a man at all. It was a very tall, humanoid creature covered in thick, matted hair. Suddenly, it started towards him.

"I took off running as fast as I could for the next light down the road," Riley said. "It was a long way off, and as I looked over my shoulder it stepped over a four foot high barbed wire fence without touching the wire." Riley knew then he was in danger. "I ran for the far-away farm house as fast as I could go. My adrenalin [was] going and [I] was scared out of my wits."

When Riley reached the farm, he jumped a perimeter fence which confined a group of farm dogs. They were barking wildly. He ran right through the pack and headed towards the house which was located some distance away. When he got to the porch, he pounded furiously on the door. He could see the owner inside, but the owner refused to open it.

When Riley looked back across the farm, he saw the creature headed towards the same pasture it had come from with the dogs now in pursuit. "That was the last I saw of it," Riley concluded. At that point he ran and hid behind a tree until things settled down.

It wasn't until 1996 that he was able to research Bigfoot sightings in Missouri. He was stunned to find so many sightings

Hills and farmland surrounding the town of Louisiana
(Photo by Lyle Blackburn)

of Momo had occurred in the very same area.

Around the time Riley was chased by an upright hairy creature, John Mayer seemingly turned the tables when he and a fellow camp counselor ended up chasing a large, bipedal entity through the woods near Potosi, Missouri. Though the location is almost 150 miles south of Louisiana, it's worth including because of the eerie similarities between his incident and what had been reported up and down the Mississippi River bank during the very same time period.

I first became aware of Mayer's incident when I did a presentation at a library in Missouri. After announcing that I was working on a book about Momo, John's wife, Angie, put me in touch with him. He's never told many people about the incident, since most simply laughed it off. As he told me the details, however, I wasn't laughing. The story was becoming all too familiar.

Mayer told me he was working as a junior counselor for a YMCA camp during the summer of 1972. One weekend in July or August, he and another counselor took a group of kids on an overnight campout in the area of Sunnen Lake, which lies in the eastern portion of the Mark Twain National Forest. The location where they set up their tents was on the top of a hill surrounded by heavy woods at least a mile from the camp's main cabins.

On the evening in question, Mayer and the senior counselor, Art, had been sitting around the campfire with the kids, singing songs and telling ghost stories. At around 11:00 p.m., they concluded the evening and got all the campers to bed. After that, they returned to the fire to relax a few minutes before retiring themselves.

"We're just sitting at the campfire, which has died down to coals, and we're talking," Mayer told me. "There's a large group of bushes and trees behind us, and we hear something back there."

Thinking it might be an animal, Art suggested they circle both sides of the bush to see if they could flush it out.

"The bush was quite large – several car lengths – so it wasn't something you could look over or see around," Mayer continued. "So as we're coming around it, something takes off running."

Whatever it was sounded large and seemed to be running on two legs. Obviously not a small animal or even a deer. It ran a short distance into the woods and stopped.

Now the counselors began to suspect someone was messing with them. Perhaps another staff member from the main camp had followed and was trying to scare them. Art suggested they retaliate by running down whomever it was and give them a taste of their own medicine, so to speak. Mayer agreed, and upon Art's signal they began running downhill towards the suspect.

"So we start chasing this guy, running through the woods, getting torn up by branches and whatnot," Mayer said. "And we can clearly see something up ahead of us. This thing is big and definitely running on two legs. It was no deer or bear or anything like that."

The two men pursued the figure downhill, yet no matter how fast they ran they simply couldn't catch up. Whatever it was seemed to be not only faster, but far more skilled at moving through the branches and thick underbrush.

When they finally reached the bottom of the hill, the trees opened into a clearing. This gave them an even better view of the figure as it fled. They couldn't see details such as a face, but there was no doubt it was big, man-like, and running entirely upright.

"As soon as this thing hits that clearing and realizes we're still chasing it, I mean it really takes off," Mayer said. "And there's no human that can run that fast."

The counselors stopped their pursuit and watched in amazement as the thing sped across the open area before it disappeared into a thatch of dark trees beyond. As they stood panting and out of breath, they suddenly felt alarmed. If it wasn't a person, then what was it? Neither man had heard of Momo at the time, nor were they familiar with the concept of Bigfoot. It was simply something they could not explain. Since they had no guns or other protection, they thought it would be best to get back to camp as quickly as possible. So they turned and headed back up the hill.

"The weird thing was that it was huge and it was really fast through those woods," Mayer remarked. "Art was on the track team and there's no way a person could have run away from us like that. And it stunk to high heaven. It was like chasing a wet horse or something. It had that animal kind of smell to it."

When the men returned to the main camp the following afternoon, they told several others about the incident, but it was met with ridicule. After that, they simply kept the story to themselves.

"I'd say it was at least a whole year after that before I began hearing stories of something called Momo; maybe 1974 or something like that," Mayer recalled. "And I thought 'wow, that's kinda weird.' Because I don't believe in them, yet that sure matches what we saw that night."

While the possibility of a human can't be ruled out, the peculiar characteristics such as the size, speed, and strong odor leave one wondering just what it was they saw.

In a similar report from the summer of 1972, Dennis Menard and his uncle also pursued a strange creature through the woods; this time near Flint Hill, Missouri, approximately 40 miles south of the Momo epicenter. Menard, who was young at the time, was spending the summer with his aunt and uncle who owned a farm in the rural area between Flint Hill and Wentzville. On a hot July evening, they had enjoyed a late dinner and were conversing around the table when the chickens began clucking loudly in the outside coop. Thinking a coyote might be on the prowl, Menard's uncle went outside to check. Menard, who shared the story with me several years ago, said that shortly afterwards his uncle came running back into the house "eyes wide open, out of breath saying that there was a 7-8 foot massive hairy creature at the chicken coop trying to get at the chickens!" His uncle said as he approached it, the thing turned its head and body towards him before it took off running down the gravel driveway. As it ran it "dropped down on all fours for a split second, came upright, cleared a two-lane blacktop in two steps and leaped over a four-foot barbed wire fence into a cornfield, cutting a diagonal wake into the forest."

Shocked and nearly speechless, his uncle told Dennis to grab his rifle and follow him. They scrambled out the door and ran as quickly as they could to the spot where the creature had entered the cornfield. It was obvious something large had gone through there, judging from the trampled stalks. They followed the path until they reached the treeline.

"Once we reached the forest edge I went in left and my uncle to the right," Menard explained. "I went in a hundred yards or so and put my back against a tree, listening for any sounds." But it was completely silent; no insects and no movement.

As Menard waited, his uncle searched the other section of woods until he came upon some kind of footprints. He followed them for about 100 yards but became too afraid to pursue any further. The effects of the dramatic sighting had him completely shaken.

After about 45 minutes nothing else happened, so Dennis rejoined his uncle and they returned to the farmhouse. Once there, his uncle recounted what he had seen. Menard, his aunt, sister, and cousin listened intently as he described the creature in more detail. He said it stood seven or eight feet tall with a massive build and long, wavy white hair all over its body. Its arms were long and it ran on two legs with "the gracefulness of an athlete."

The whole thing sounded bizarre, but young Dennis felt certain his uncle saw what he said he saw. And Dennis knew something had run into the cornfield. He saw the trampled corn stalks himself. At the time neither he nor anyone else in his family had heard of Bigfoot or even Momo, so it wasn't something they connected. The fact that it was white seemed even more bizarre since it was even less typical of any ape-like animal they were familiar with.

Following the incident, Menard said several other farmers in the area reported seeing similar bipedal creatures, however, these were described as having brown or black hair. Perhaps these were related to the Momo case, as they matched more closely with what was being seen around Louisiana at the time. The white-furred animal was unique among these, although coincidentally an outbreak of white-haired creature sightings started up in the neighboring state of Illinois around the same time. It seemed that either more creatures were on the loose, or perhaps imitation may have been the best form of Momo flattery.

Cohomo

The corresponding monster reports in Illinois originated from the area of Pekin in Tazewell County, which sits along the Illinois River northeast of the Momo epicenter. According to articles in the *Pekin Daily Times*, the first came in July 1972 from Randy Emert, a young man who claimed he had seen a huge, hairy creature on Cole Hollow Road twice since May.[43] He said it was mostly white in color and stood at least eight feet tall. The thing moved very quickly and let out "a long screech kinda like an old steam engine whistle, only more human." It also left three-toed footprints.

Emert's report was followed by others. On July 27, an unidentified woman told the Tazewell County Sheriff's Office she had seen the same — or a similar creature — while picking berries near an old coal mine. It scared her so bad she dropped everything and ran.[44]

In nearby Peoria, police received an equally strange report from a man who said he and his family spotted two unidentified lights in the sky around 8:30 p.m. He said they moved vertically and went down behind some trees. As they did, they left a "vapor or smoke trail." Peoria police also said "two reliable citizens" claimed to have seen a very tall "Momo type creature" which "looked like a cross between an ape and a cave man."

The Tazewell County Sheriff's Office ended up receiving quite a few calls of a similar nature which seemed to echo the Momo frenzy. Reporters even concocted a name for the beast, calling it the Cole Hollow Road Monster or "Cohomo" for short. By all accounts Cohomo was a more monstrous version of Momo, covered in whitish hair, standing up to ten feet tall, and having a red mouth with sharp teeth.

Though the police fielded numerous calls and even organized a search with at least 100 volunteers, the Cohomo sightings were not documented in as much detail nor covered by as many news outlets as in the Momo case. Not to mention, the description of a ten-foot white creature with a red mouth seemed a bit suspect — even by Momo standards. Years later Randy Emert called the *Peoria Journal Star* newspaper and said he and his friends made up the story about the creature "to scare another friend who worked late nights at a gas station" at the top of Cole Hollow Road.[45] Somehow this doesn't seem too surprising, although it doesn't explain the conviction of the other Cohomo witnesses that followed. And, as DeWayne Bartels points out in a retrospective article published by the *East Peoria Times-Courier*: "If Cohomo was the product of mass hallucination, caused by the sightings of a Missouri monster called Momo, why did only the citizens of Tazewell County invent the elusive beast?"[46]

Strange things were definitely happening in 1972, and the wider the scope became, the stranger they got.

Periphery of Mystery

While much of the Momo case seems to fall into the category of "Bigfoot" with its profile of a hairy, bipedal hominid, it occupies other realms of the paranormal by virtue of the unidentified lights and disembodied voices reported in conjunction with the creature sightings. Whether these things were connected or purely coincidental is a matter of conjecture, but there's no doubt they added to the atmosphere of mystery.

The first of the peripheral phenomenon was experienced by Edgar Harrison and his fellow church parishioners on July 14, when they saw the green and white balls of light prior to hearing the loud growling sound. Growling seems indicative of an animal,

One of the bluffs near the town of Louisiana
(Photo by Lyle Blackburn)

but Harrison said they heard another loud noise just before the growling. He described it as a "ringing noise," which could be compared to rocks being thrown at a metal water reservoir, not unlike the one which stood atop Marzolf Hill.[47] After an "especially loud ring" he heard the growling, which then prompted his family to flee the scene.

Details of these particular noises and lights were sprinkled in the newsprint amid accounts of the creature, while other similarly strange activities were later documented by Richard Crowe. According to Crowe, on the night of July 26 witnesses reported seeing a "fireball" land or hover atop a large tree near the railroad crossing on River Road, not far from where Ellis Minor claimed to have seen the creature. They said "two red spurts of light shot out from it" before it zoomed out of sight.[48]

For the next three nights, witnesses – including members of the Harrison family and the Shade family – saw more colored lights above a bluff at the north end of River Road. These lights appeared to be "signaling back and forth" to each other.[49] Mrs. Lois Shade (Edgar Harrison's sister) estimated they were "about the size of an apple."

The Shade family seemed quite lucky as far as aerial phenomenon goes. On Sunday July 30, they saw yet another strange light or craft hovering over a thicket at the top of another bluff. Earnest Shade (Lois' husband) described it as being orange at first, then later changing to red and gray. Lois Shade said "it was disc-shaped" and had what appeared to be lighted "windows."[50] The UFO remained there for several hours then suddenly gave off a "red glow" before it "went straight up into the air and disappeared."

More weirdness of the audible kind occurred on the night of August 5, when Pat Howard (who saw a dark, man-like figure on the morning of July 15) and a friend were camping in the Harrison's backyard (presumably on the lookout for Momo). As they sipped coffee, they heard a strange voice say: "I'll take a cup of your coffee." They conducted an immediate search of the area, but couldn't find anyone. The disembodied voice was reminiscent of the one reported by Harrison and the college students a few weeks earlier.

The terrible stench was also a topic of debate. Harrison noted that the smell was always apparent "just when the searchers were onto something." He felt it might be a tactic used to distract them. According to Richard Crowe, the Texas sailors were searching the area for themselves when they reportedly saw a "small glowing light that silently exploded and was followed by the stench."[51] Harrison confirmed he had seen something similar.

As reports of unidentified lights, creepy sounds, and bizarre odors continued, a growing number of UFO researchers pointed out that skyward activity during that time was not confined to the town of Louisiana. Similar incidents were being reported in and around the Mississippi basin both in Missouri and in neighboring states such as Illinois.

On July 11, the same day Momo appeared on the Harrison property, an unidentified flying object was reported in Decatur, Illinois, 120 miles to the east. The object, described as the "size of a star," moved in an unusual manner as it was observed by a witness for nearly four minutes.[52]

On July 14, the same night the green and white lights were seen by the residents of Louisiana, UFOs were reported in New Canton, Illinois.[53] New Canton is a mere 13 miles to the north across the Mississippi River.

A week later, on July 21, something very similar to the Momo-related events was reported in Bowling Green, Missouri, only 12 miles from the town of Louisiana. In this case, a housewife said she observed "two balls of fire land in a cow pasture near her home."[54] Later, she smelled a "nauseating odor" followed by a series of "grunting and screaming noises" which were also heard by her entire family. They said it was unlike anything they'd ever heard before.

In a rundown of the Momo events published in the September 1972 edition of *Skylook*, the official publication of the Midwest UFO Network, editor Norma Short pointed out that while she didn't personally see a connection between the creature and the strange lights, a number of her colleagues did. The publication went on to recount a dramatic UFO sighting which occurred in St. Louis County on July 22. That evening, around 8:30 p.m., three children were playing outside their home when they noticed a strange object in the sky. It descended from the north, "then hovered and appeared to rotate slowly as it launched separately five smaller objects."[55] The larger object was shaped like a "football" and was gold in color, while the smaller ones were round and white. The objects hovered for a few seconds before they all dispersed in different directions.

UFO reports from young children are hardly reliable, but they weren't the only observers. Local radio station KXOK received a total of 13 calls that night from various people who reported seeing similar unexplained lights in the sky. In one case, two callers said they'd seen it over a football field only a mile from where the children lived. Calls to local airbases and government officials did not turn up any official activity of weather balloons or other man-made craft in the area.

The connection between Bigfoot-like creatures and UFOs, if any, has been hotly debated among paranormal researchers over the years. While the majority of Bigfoot-type sightings occur without any corresponding UFO activity, there are cases where unusual lights and flying objects are seen within the same vicinity and time period, causing some to speculate that the creature – or creatures – in question may have originated from some type of alien spacecraft.

One of the most significant flaps of simultaneous Bigfoot/UFO activity occurred in Pennsylvania at the same time the Momo mayhem was taking place. The Pennsylvania activity was documented by my colleague and notable researcher, Stan Gordon, who writes about it extensively in his book *Silent Invasion*. According to Gordon, strange events were first reported during April 1972 in Westmoreland County, located at the southwest corner of the state. In this case, numerous people observed "glowing spheres of light" or "formations of glowing objects" in the sky.[56] Along with the UFO incidents came eyewitness sightings and dramatic encounters with large, ape-like creatures not unlike what was being reported in Missouri.

Residents near Greensburg in Pennsylvania's Westmoreland County first began to notice strange "screaming sounds bellowing from the woods" in May of 1972.[57] Not long after, two people were walking near an old cemetery one morning when they saw a dark-colored creature with very broad shoulders chasing two dogs. Later, in July, an unidentified glowing object was seen flying over the cemetery. The UFO reportedly "made a ninety degree

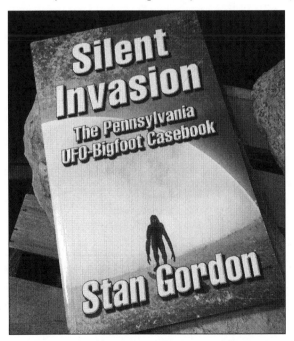

Silent Invasion, book by Stan Gordon

turn and moved off in the distance."

Several months later, a strange animal was seen near the town of Latrobe east of Greensburg. Witnesses said they were driving along when they noticed an animal "similar to a chimpanzee" standing on two legs near a guard rail. The creature was dark in color, and when the vehicle approached it crawled over the rail and disappeared from sight. Another set of witnesses told state police that a creature which looked like a "gorilla" had walked on two legs across the highway in front of their car in the same area.

At the south end of Westmoreland County, a large, hairy creature was seen on multiple occasions outside a rural home. The family members initially tried to convince themselves it was just a bear, but the fact that it was man-like in form and walked upright, just didn't sit right. After several fleeting glimpses, their worst fears were confirmed. On that evening, several members of the family noticed a "dark man-like shape" standing in the yard, so they grabbed a shotgun and headed out to confront it. Surprisingly, the thing stood still as the group approached within six feet. Now they could see it definitely wasn't a bear. "The creature looked like a hefty built man and stood about six-and-a-half feet tall," Gordon noted.[58] It was covered in dark hair with broad shoulders and long arms. It was standing upright, "just like a man." One of the witnesses became so frightened, the whole group retreated to the house. They could only watch as the creature finally slipped off into the darkness.

A short time later, a UFO was sighted on the north end of Westmoreland County. A local resident said he was driving to work early one morning when he noticed a "strange object resting on an uncut grass field." It was so unusual and out of place, he pulled over to get a better look. He described it as an "oblong triangular" object approximately fifty feet in length with a "pyramid shaped dome at the top." It was illuminated by orange lights, which oddly enough didn't reflect on the grass beneath it. The object may have been hovering, but it was hard to tell for sure. The witness watched for a few moments until he became so unnerved, he pulled his car back onto the road and sped off.

Incidents like these continued well into the following year, some mirroring other characteristics of the Momo case. For example, on August 20, 1973, a number of large, unidentified tracks were found in the woods outside of Irwin, Pennsylvania.[59] They measured 13 inches long and appeared to have three toes! Both Gordon's investigative team and local police examined the tracks and concluded that if they were a hoax, it was very well done.

Strange smells were also reported amid the flying objects and apes. On August 29, a woman said she detected an odd sulfur-like odor after she saw a "large, solid boomerang-shaped object with windows" fly overhead.[60] That same night she also heard gunshots. The next day she learned the shots had been fired by a doctor who lived a short distance away. He said his dogs were barking uncontrollably, so he went outside to check on them. When he got outside, he was shocked to see some kind of "big ape" moving across his property. He retrieved a rifle from inside the house and tried to shoot it, but it managed to run off into the woods unscathed.

The "Bigfoot" reports eventually garnered so much news in the Latrobe area, it affected the culture much like Momo did in Missouri. Local businesses made the best of it by offering Bigfoot Burgers and Bigfoot-related specials, while local radio stations dedicated talk shows to the subject. Law enforcement officials even formed the obligatory posse to scour the woods along what is known as the Chestnut Ridge. The ridge, which is the westernmost portion of the Allegheny Mountains, seemed to be the focus of much of the strange activity.

In the end, however, proof remained elusive, and Gordon and his associates were left to ponder whether there was any connection between the flying objects and hairy creatures being reported in proximity. As with Momo, the situation had plenty of circumstantial and anecdotal evidence, but there was no way to make a solid conclusion either way. No one saw Momo or any of the other alleged entities actually getting on or off a spacecraft, so the possibility these were extraterrestrial creatures tread in as much muddy water as other possibilities, such as an elaborate hoax or an unknown ape. If it were an undocumented ape, it was perhaps just as coincidental that the Momo sightings occurred in an area where rumors of such a creature had been quietly circulating since the halcyon days of Tom Sawyer and Huckleberry Finn.

Chapter 3.

HAIR, THERE, AND EVERYWHERE

In many ways Louisiana and the surrounding area exemplify the heart of early rural America as portrayed in Mark Twain's classic tales of Tom Sawyer and Huck Finn. This is not at all surprising since Twain (a.k.a. Samuel Langhorne Clemens) was born and raised in the town of Hannibal, Missouri, a mere 30 miles north of Louisiana. Hannibal would later serve as the setting for both *The Adventures of Tom Sawyer* (1875) and its sequel, *Adventures of Huckleberry Finn* (1885), which is often praised as "The Great American Novel." One has only to read these classic works to get a sense of the antebellum society and the importance of the river to these townships in their early days.

Like Hannibal, Louisiana is nestled within a backdrop of rolling hills and river culture. During the time of the Momo sightings, the town's population was around 4,500, which places it firmly within the definition of "Small Town America." Louisiana was founded in 1816 by an enterprising settler, John Walter Basye, who previously lived in St. Louis where French culture was prominent. At the suggestion of a friend, Basye named the town after his daughter, Louisiana Basye, who was born around the same time. Other early residents included Samuel Caldwell and Joel Shaw, both of whom purchased land from Bayse in 1818. All three properties became the original town plat, comprised primarily of land on the riverfront.[61]

Earlier settlers first began moving into the region shortly

after the Louisiana Purchase was made by the United States in 1803. The area was attractive due to its rich land and proximity to the waterway. Native Americans, who were already living in the area, also valued the land and resisted the intrusion with violence. To protect its citizens, the American military constructed a strategic fort two miles south of the present day town of Louisiana. Fort Buffalo, as it was called, was built in 1811 and was instrumental in defending the early settlers from the Sauk and Fox tribes who eventually sided with the British in the War of 1812.[62]

Once the war was settled, Louisiana began to prosper. Its position on the Mississippi made it a premium spot for the burgeoning river trade and commerce. Industries such as grain and lumber moved in first, followed by manufacturers of tools, clothes, and tobacco in the coming years. Missouri achieved statehood in 1821 as early Americans continued to venture westward, Louisiana being one of the earliest established settlements in the

Welcome to historic Louisiana, Missouri
(Photo by Lyle Blackburn)

area. Steamboats could always be seen moving up and down the river and by 1871, the railroad also arrived. Clarksville and Western routed tracks along the river bank, while a rotating "swing bridge" was built across the water to Illinois. It was one of the first railroad bridges constructed over the Mississippi, and it's one of only two swing bridges still in operation on the river today.

As the town's commerce continued to boom, so did its population. By the end of the 1800s, Louisiana's modest census had risen to over 7,000 people. Their wealth and prosperity were reflected in the lavish Victorian style homes which began to dot the landscape. The downtown district also reflected the era of riverboat and railroad prosperity with buildings that featured Italianate or Greek Revival architectural. Many of these homes and businesses have been preserved, and in 1987 the town's Georgia

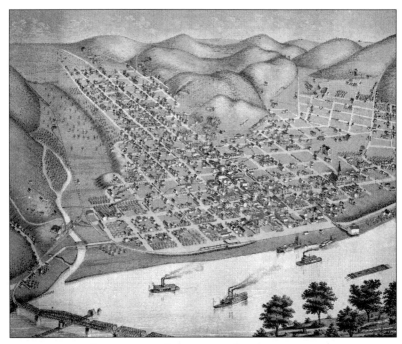

Bird's-Eye View of the town of Louisiana in 1876
(Credit: Library of Congress Archives[65])

Street Historic District was added to the National Register of Historic Places.[63]

In the midst of all this stands Marzolf Hill, whose strange story looms as large as the Victorian streetscape below. The hill derived its name from George Marzolf, a German immigrant who helped shape the prosperity of Louisiana in its early years. Marzolf moved to Louisiana in 1861 where he began a grocery business with John Seibert. The partners eventually closed the grocery business and began manufacturing plug tobacco in 1846, and later cigars under the company name of Marzolf & Siebert. From 1866 to 1867 Marzolf also served as a Louisiana town councilman. As a testament to his contribution, the hill still bears his surname.[64]

In the 1930s, Marzolf Hill also became known as "Star Hill" due to a lighted star placed there annually during the Christmas season. The star, which was constructed of wood, contained 130 individual lights and stood nearly 40 feet tall. The Missouri Edison Company first displayed it on the hill in 1931 where it could be seen from almost anywhere in town, and even for miles around.[66] The fact the hill would later become associated with a "monster" is amusing, considering its original tradition as a beloved yuletide focal point.

In terms of mysteries and oddities, Momo is not Louisiana's only claim to fame. Residents still talk about the mystery of the Clark Theater Bombing, an apparent crime that went unsolved. The theater, which was located at 316 Georgia Street, opened May 22, 1931. The theater was to be a new hub of social activity with its modern architecture and inviting atmosphere, until misfortune struck. Just a few days after its opening, a huge explosion rocked Georgia Street, shattering every window on the block. Several buildings were damaged, but it was the Clark Theater that suffered the most devastation. To the horror of investigators, it appeared the lobby of the Clark had been the detonation point for a bomb. An intense investigation was launched, but to this day neither the

Destruction at the Clark Theater in 1931
(Credit: Cinema Treasures)

perpetrator(s) nor a motive has ever been uncovered.

At the 100 block of Georgia Street stands the infamous "Leaning House." The house – which was actually a saloon – appears to be leaning at a considerable angle. This is an optical illusion, however. The structure was built level, but due to the road's particular slant it appears as though it's about to fall over. The appearance is so striking, it was featured in a 1940s issue of National Geographic magazine!

Geographically, Louisiana is located at the eastern end of Pike County, named in recognition of one of America's preeminent explorers, Zebulon Pike. (Pike not only surveyed the upper northern reaches of the Mississippi River on behalf of President

Thomas Jefferson, but ventured into Colorado where the famous Pike's Peak also bears his surname.) Pike and a number of other Missouri counties to the north, south, and west are all part of the Interior River Valleys and Hills ecosystem which spreads in a Y-shape along the confluence of the Mississippi and Missouri Rivers just north of the Ozarks. The geology here is mottled with bluffs, valleys, and lows hills which channel a maze of perennial streams and rivers.[67] Limestone, sandstone, and shale rock formations combine with areas of exposed bedrock to create a variety of karst features such as caves and overhangs. In terms of land cover, the area contains rich croplands, pastures, and vast vegetation comprised of oak woodlands and sugar maple-oak forests. The River Valley ecosystem provides an ideal habit for a variety of creatures who take advantage of its shelter, forestry, waterways, and proximity to agricultural crops.

Judging from the reports, the Momo sightings took place

Landscape along the Mississippi River Valley
(Photo by Lyle Blackburn)

in all of these terrains including woods, pastures, hills, and even water. Marzolf Hill is located within city limits, yet it's less than a mile from the Mississippi River and the Ted Shanks Conservation Area, a forested belt bordered by the Mississippi River to the east and the Salt River to the west. North of Shanks lies two other conservation areas made up of forests and river islands formed by the Mississippi.

While central Missouri isn't the first place that comes to mind in terms of Bigfoot, waterways such as the Mississippi have an undeniable association with Bigfoot sightings when plotted on a map. It seems that wherever these creatures are sighted, water is not far away, whether it's a lake, swamp, creek, or river. Perhaps this is not coincidental since such a massive creature would require a high intake of water in order to survive. Not to mention, areas with water and high annual rainfall tend to have the most vegetation, and therefore the most cover in which to potentially hide.

Stories of bipedal, ape-like creatures have been quietly circulating along this stretch of the Mississippi River for at least 50 years. According to John Green in his book *Sasquatch: The Apes Among Us*, a woman told reporters in 1970 that hunters and trappers in the area of Maquoketa, Iowa, spoke of "animals that walked like men."[68] The article explained: "It is the mysterious creature folks around here have heard about for 50 years — a furry, scary thing that stands like a man." Coincidently, Maquoketa is located directly north of Missouri along the Mississippi River.

The mention of these older stories was prompted by an incident which occurred in 1966. That year, Gary Koontz of Maquoketa, Iowa, was hunting in the dense woods north of the "state park" when he spotted a strange creature at a close distance of about 100 feet. (Presumably, this would be Bellevue State Park which is located on the western bank of the Mississippi near Maquoketa.) Koontz said it was standing upright, about 4-5 feet tall, with dark fur or hair, and a flat face.

"I knew it was something I had never seen before," Koontz explained.[69] "I was startled but decided to take a shot at it with my shotgun and I'm sure I hit it. It let out a high-pitched, woman-like scream and disappeared into the brush."

Koontz was too afraid to follow the injured creature, but if he had, perhaps he would have been the first to prove a long-standing Midwest mystery.

Blue Man and the Wild Ones

Across the wilds of the Show-Me State, stories of similar feral, man-like creatures date back even further. One of the oldest is that of the "Blue Man," a hairy, human-looking thing said to roam the Ozarks area in southern Missouri. According to a 1915 article from the *Kansas City Star*, the first sighting occurred in the spring of 1865 when 60-year-old resident Blue Sol Collins was out hunting.[70] A light snow had fallen the previous night and an abundance of animal tracks were visible on the ground. Collins had intended to hunt deer, but when he noticed a set of huge, clawed tracks resembling that of a bear, he decided to pursue the larger game instead.

After hours of tracking, Collins was beginning to lose hope when he finally spotted something climbing on the north slope of Upper Twin Mountain. He was certain it was the maker of the tracks, but it was definitely not a bear. It was a giant figure that looked very human-like although its body was covered in "blue-black hair." Collins said it was nearly seven feet in height with a powerful, muscular build and "gorilla-like arms." It wore a shoulder piece and breech-cloth of animal skin, while its feet were covered with "deer hide moccasins, held together by thongs of buckskin that made the clawlike appearance in the snow." It also held a huge club in its hand. When it spotted Collins, it began to hurl rocks. The hunter was so frightened, he turned and ran for home.

Collins never saw the Blue Man again, but others claimed to have had encounters between 1874 and 1890 in the vicinity of Douglas County, just a few miles south and east of Springfield in an area that remains wild, heavily forested and vastly unpopulated to this day. In one instance, a man said he came across the thing as it was carrying a calf near North Fork. When the creature saw the man, it began to chase him as it let out a roar. Others claimed to have seen it in Spring Creek Hills where it was apparently stealing livestock from the local farmers.

A drought of sightings between 1890 and 1910 caused many to speculate that the Blue Man was dead, but in 1911 a posse of men supposedly discovered the creature's cave and set a "large saw-toothed bear trap" inside. When they returned a few days later, it appeared the Blue Man had been snared but had escaped by cutting off two of its fingers.

In 1915, the creature was spotted again at his old haunt in Spring Creek Hills when a man by the name of O.C. Collins saw it trying to catch a hog. Collins said the Blue Man's hair was now white, possibly due to old age.

While details such as a breech-cloth, footwear, and use of a club seem indicative of a human, the subject was consistently reported as having a covering of dark hair or fur. The notion that its hair eventually turned white may seem odd, but as we've already seen, white hair is occasionally associated with Bigfoot creatures.

A decade before the Blue Man was first sighted, an article from the May 9, 1851 edition of *The Memphis Enquirer* recounted the story of a Sasquatch-like creature in Greene County, Arkansas, some 30 miles south of the Missouri line, nestled up to the "bootheel" of the state. According to the article, two men were out hunting when they saw a tall, hairy man-like animal chasing after some cattle. "He was of gigantic stature, the body being covered with hair and the head with long locks that fairly enveloped his neck and shoulders," the article stated.[71] The "wildman," as it was called, looked briefly at the hunters, then "turned and ran away with great speed, leaping from twelve to fourteen feet at a time." After the thing was gone they located some interesting footprints it left behind. The prints weren't overly massive, yet still measured 13 inches long.

In 1881, the *Iron County Register* reported on two strange incidents which occurred in the heavy forests west of Ironton, Missouri. In the first incident, a man named Strickland was out hunting with his dogs when he noticed an animal laying in a pile of leaves. Thinking it was perhaps a "domestic animal," he continued walking. As he got closer, however, the thing stood up on two feet and faced him.

"The [thing] had the face of a human being and was entirely without clothing," he said. "Its body was covered with long dark hair, which streamed in the cool wind, like the mane of a horse."[72]

After it stood up, the strange beast immediately took off running. Strickland's first thought was to shoot it, but he hesitated and by then it was out of range. His hunting dogs took up the chase, but Strickland quickly called them back. Whatever the thing was, he felt it was best to let it go. The newspaper noted that he considered organizing a search party at a later date – presumably to capture it – but never followed through.

A month later, the thing was presumably seen again, this time by two people. A young couple said they were walking home from a small, isolated church house when a "strange hairy beast" jumped out in front of them. It waved its arms in a bizarre fashion as the girl screamed in terror. After a few moments it simply disappeared into the woods.

Creatures such as these were commonly referred to as "wild men" in those days, as they incorporated features of both animal and man – not unlike Bigfoot. The accounts appear in a number of old newspapers from the 1800s, including some from Missouri. Their prominence was enough to capture the attention of the aforementioned Mark Twain, who made a satirical statement about the subject in the September 18, 1869, edition of the *Buffalo Express* newspaper. In an article titled "The Wild Man Interviewed," Twain writes:

> *There has been so much talk about the mysterious "wild man" out there in the West for some time, that I finally felt it was my duty to go out and interview him. There was something peculiarly and touchingly romantic about the creature and his strange actions, according to the newspaper reports. He was represented as being hairy, long-armed, and of great strength and stature; ugly and cumbrous; avoiding men, but appearing suddenly and unexpectedly to women and children; going armed with a club, but never molesting any creature, except sheep, or other prey; fond of eating and drinking, and not particular about the quality, quantity, or character of the beverages and edibles; living in the woods like a wild beast, but never angry; moaning, and sometimes howling, but never uttering articulate sounds.[73]*

Twain follows this opening statement with a fictional interview "conducted" with a wild man he calls Old Shep. Among other things, Old Shep proceeds to "tell" Twain that he's been around throughout all of human history before bemoaning his current state as puppet for the journalistic whims of "crazy newspaper scribblers." While this doesn't shed an ounce of light on the authenticity of the wild men in question, I figured it was worth mentioning as part of Missouri culture and hairy-beast history. It's also interesting because the location where Strickland and the young couple claimed to have seen the wild man type animal is now known as the Mark Twain National Forest. Ironic to say the least!

On June 19, 1891, the *Hornellsville Weekly Tribune* provides the details of yet another wild man sighting north of Alex-

One of the many entrances into the Mark Twain National Forest (Photo by Michael Rocco)

andria, Missouri. In this case, the wild man had been seen on the outskirts of the city where he "badly frightened women and children."[74] He (or it) was described as being a creature with a "shaggy beard, ferocious cast of countenance, and matted white hair." The wild man was said to be "almost naked" except for a small red blanket thrown over the shoulder. Locals tried to capture him, but were unsuccessful.

Another story popped up three years later in *The Hamilton Daily Republican* newspaper. In this case, a wild man was seen roaming around a creek and some blackberry patches in the hills south of Sedalia, Missouri. According to witnesses: "The wild man is a shaggy, ferocious-looking individual over six feet six inches tall and clad in rags, with long matted hair."[75] The wild man apparently avoided contact with people. Witnesses reported "he bounds away like a deer at the sight of anyone."

The standard search was made by the locals, during which

they discovered a cave near the creek. Inside they found what looked to be a bed made from leaves. "Among the leaves were several heavy sticks, worn smooth from much handling, the article stated. "Scattered around on the ground were a lamb's skin, parts of rabbits and squirrels, and a number of hog's ears." They believed the wild man had been living in the cave, however, he was nowhere to be found. The article ends by saying another hunt would ensue, this time using bloodhounds.

Such stories continued into the early twentieth century. According to an article in the June 26, 1925, edition of the *Standard* – a newspaper from Mountain View, Missouri – there had been three sightings of an alleged hairy, man-like creature near the town of Alton, just north of the Arkansas border. One man, who got within 50 yards of the thing, described it as "an animal that walks upright like a man, rather brown hair all over and had a face something like a monkey."[76]

A subsequent article in the *Standard* proposed the "animal" may have actually been a transient who was in the area at the time. Police in Chillicothe questioned the individual in August when he was passing through their town. The sheriff said he was wearing clothes, but underneath he had "a six-inch growth of matted hair" on his body. The transient admitted to having passed through the Alton area a month prior, although no explanation was given as to why he would have been wearing no clothes at the time. As well, his hair was black, not brown as described by the Alton witnesses.

Given these type of details, it's often unclear as to whether the subject is more of an upright, hairy *creature* or simply a ragged human, perhaps one living in a feral state. As reports progressed in the twentieth century, however, they became decidedly more in favor of the former. It was a pattern that built a quiet backstory for the coming age of Momo.

Show-Me Bigfoot

One of the earliest Missouri-based Bigfoot stories dates back to 1932. The story was recounted by Will Rowen, who said his parents encountered a Bigfoot-like creature on several occasions while his father was working at a logging camp near St. Joseph in Buchanan County around that time.[77] The first report of the strange creature came from the wife of a fellow logger, who said she saw a "hairy, man like beast" one night while sitting on the back porch of their cabin. As it approached, she screamed and it retreated into the woods. When she told everyone at the camp about the sighting, including his parents, they reacted with laughter. A short time later, however, nobody was laughing.

Around dusk, Rowen's father and mother were sitting outside when they saw the creature come out of the woods and approach their truck which was parked about 200 feet from their cabin. They described it as being "bigger than a man" with "hair all over its body." The closest thing they could compare it to was a "gorilla," although it was clearly not.

The thing began to come around the logging cabins with more frequency and eventually it was seen by several other witnesses. "They said it would run upright and very fast," Rowen recalled. "The dogs would chase it sometimes and it would just outrun the dogs quickly."

Once the loggers realized they were dealing with an unknown creature, naturally they wanted to shoot it. However, Rowen's father convinced them otherwise. In his opinion, it looked "too much like a human."

At the time, the concept of Bigfoot in North America was simply unknown. Yet whatever it was they saw, it undoubtedly falls into the Bigfoot category. Rowen confirmed that his father, who later became a Baptist Minister, was not one to joke around. His parents both recounted the story on many occasions and assured him it was true.

Years later, in May 1966, Larry Lawhon and five others tried to hunt down a man-like animal who frightened some "youngsters" in the same woods surrounding St. Joseph.[78] During the pursuit, the "dark shape" of the creature was seen by all the men, including Lawhon who said it passed within 30 yards. He could only describe it as a "bigfoot-like thing," at least nine feet tall with "short black hair."

According to news reports in the 1940s, an animal which looked "something like a gorilla" was reportedly shot to death after ripping a cow apart in southeast Missouri. The creature, they said, had been known to kill full-grown cows and horses, leaving their uneaten corpses to rot in the nearby swamps.[79]

In 1947 a hairy, man-thing allegedly tore through the Piney Ridge area of Pulaski County, Missouri. It started when coon hunters chased a strange animal after it was caught killing sheep and goats owned by Martin Burford.[80] A man named Glen Payne

The dense woods of the Ozarks
(Photo by Lyle Blackburn)

also attempted to run it down with the aid of his "hog dogs." Payne described it as "a giant hairy man-shaped thing." The dogs finally caught up with it, but the situation took a turn for the worse when the beast killed the dogs, and supposedly, overturned Payne's jeep.

Two rather chilling sightings originate from Pemiscot County which is located on the banks of the Mississippi River in southern Missouri. The first occurred in August 1960 near Caruthersville. The witness in this case said that when he was young his family moved to a home in the woods which had been abandoned for quite some time. Not long after they moved in, he was sitting on the front porch with his younger brother while his sister was playing near the barn about 75 yards away.

"I heard my sister scream and start crying," the witness recalled. "I looked to the barn as a large creature stood there."[81] It was at least a foot taller than the top of the barn door, which would make it over seven feet tall. It was covered in hair, massively built, and had long arms.

The witness watched with a mix of concern and amazement as the thing turned and walked to the east with long, fluid strides. It easily stepped over a fence which kept the hogs penned and walked away into the distance. After the children had calmed, the witness ventured to the barn to investigate.

"I was over by the barn and saw the large footprints replete with toe marks," he reported. "Over the remaining time we lived in that house, through the next spring, we heard loud noises at times coming from the metal grain silos to the west of the barn. Though, we never saw the creature again."

The second sighting is said to have occurred one year later in Hornersville, only a few miles east of Caruthersville. According to the witness in this case, as a boy he was playing outside his home one evening when he noticed his dog had gone over to their old barn and was sniffing back and forth in the weeds. A few seconds later, the dog began to bark in a fearful manner, causing enough concern that the witness starting walking towards the dog. Before he could make it all the way to the barn, however, the dog turned and ran toward him.

"He came running out toward me very fast and then I saw why," the witness recalled.[82] "Right behind him was the biggest thing." It looked to be some sort of ape-like creature, yet it stood on two legs. It was bulky, tall and covered in "very dark brownish, nearly black, bushy hair" with huge, outstretched hands.

"I stopped in my tracks," the witness recalled. "Then he saw me and did the same. We were looking right at each other, eye to eye." The thing was no more than ten feet away as the young witness stood looking, trying to grasp just what kind of person or animal it was. It didn't look "completely animal but also not completely human in its actions and appearance."

After a few confused moments, the witness turned and ran towards his parents' house as fast as he could with his dog close behind. The creature didn't give chase and was gone by the time he reached the home. The witness rushed inside and frantically told his parents what he'd seen, but as he put it, "they did not believe a word of it." To this day, he himself cannot explain it except in terms of Bigfoot.

In July 1968, a "bear-like animal" reportedly came from the woods near St. Louis and grabbed a four-year-old boy as he was playing in the backyard.[83] The child's aunt, who was watching him at the time, screamed as the thing began to carry the child towards the woods. The family's dog started after it, barking and growling. Fortunately, the thing decided to drop the boy just before it disappeared into the trees. The police were summoned, and upon hearing the story, immediately launched a search of the woods behind the house. However, they found no sign of the animal, tracks or otherwise. Whatever it was, it apparently resembled something like a cross between a bear and a "gorilla."

Just two years prior to the first Momo sighting, a woman claimed to have seen something with a definite ape-like anatomy run across the road in Paris, Missouri, just a few counties west of Pike County. It was July 1969 at around 10:30 p.m. when she and her boyfriend were driving back from a visit with his aunt. As they drove through a rural wooded area, suddenly a "furry ape like animal came up out of the ditch on the left side of the road," she told an investigator for the Gulf Coast Bigfoot Research Organization (GCBRO).[84] The animal proceeded to run across the road in clear view of the headlights, swinging its long arms and staying upright on two legs as it went.

"It was dark colored with thick fur," the woman noted, and was "taller than the front end of the car." When it ran across the road, which was about 30 feet wide, it ran somewhat diagonally with a better view of its back side rather than its front. At that angle, the couple could not see its face.

After the animal reached the ditch on the other side of the road, the boyfriend stopped the vehicle and jumped out. He tried to get another look at it, but it had gone into the dark woods beyond the road and disappeared from sight.

The woman insisted they were completely sober at the time and were certain it was a bipedal primate at least three feet tall, judging by the height of the car hood. She stressed that she grew up on a farm in central Missouri and knew the local wildlife. "I know the difference between raccoons, opossums, cats, brown bears, skunks, groundhogs, etc. I had NEVER seen anything like this before and haven't since," she explained.

As her boyfriend was looking for it in the darkness, the thought crossed her mind that perhaps it was a baby and a much larger mother could be nearby. "I yelled for him to come back to the car," she said. "After that I had nightmares of these animals living in the woods near the 'Union Covered Bridge' now a State Historical site."

The alarming creature was obviously smaller and more primate-like than what witnesses would report in Pike County a few years later, but nonetheless it adds another furry anecdote to the widening Momo mystery.

Icy Corpses

One of the strangest stories I've come across in relation to the Momo case is that of a frozen body seen nearly a decade before the frenzy. The details came from Judy Gustin, whom I met while doing a presentation at a Bigfoot event in Oklahoma. Judy is a well-spoken woman who's had a keen interest in the Bigfoot phenomenon since an early age. We first discussed our mutual interest in the Fouke Monster (Boggy Creek) case. Amazingly enough, her family had taken a trip to Fouke, Arkansas, during the 1970s in response to the frenzy going on there at the time. As we began to talk about other interesting cases, she mentioned she'd seen a frozen body of a Bigfoot-like creature in Missouri back in 1964. Frozen body? 1964? My interest was piqued to say the least.

Judy explained that she was 25 years old when she, her husband, and a group of their friends were on their way to a local lake. As they passed through the town of Joplin, Missouri, they noticed a crowd of people gathered around a truck trailer in the parking lot of a shopping mall. There appeared to be an exhibit on display; some sort of "missing link" frozen in a block of ice. The trailer was plain and unmarked, but several signs placed around it advertised the alleged contents.

I politely interjected, thinking I knew where the story was headed. "Was it the Minnesota Iceman?" I asked. I assumed it was the rather well-known sideshow exhibit which began making rounds in the late 1960s.

"I don't think so," she said. "This thing was supposedly shot near Louisiana, Missouri."

Louisiana, Missouri? I was stunned.

She continued the story, explaining that the exhibit was so appealing she convinced the group to stop so she could take a look. The entry fee was one dollar, so she gladly paid and waited in line along with several other customers. No cameras or other such items were allowed inside the exhibit, so she left her purse with her husband.

After a few minutes, the group was permitted to enter the trailer. Once inside, they gathered around a large, rectangular freezer unit which was filled with a solid block of ice. Judy peered into it with amazement. There, frozen in the ice just below the surface, was something that resembled a primitive, hair-covered man. It was lying face up with its arms extended downward and its hands covering the crotch area. On its chest, she could see what appeared to be a gunshot wound with a hint of pinkish ice, as if the wound had bled a little during the freezing process. Its mouth was frozen in a rictus grin, revealing human-like teeth, and its eyes were partially open, gazing upward at Judy through the cloudy ice. The whole thing looked amazingly real, and Judy was convinced it was.

"It resembled a crude human," Judy told me. "It was in the largest size chest freezer. The freezer was actually a little short for it so it was crammed in there. You could see a large caliber bullet hole in its chest. It definitely looked like it had been shot. I wouldn't have called it an animal, but I wouldn't have called it a human either."

She examined the entire display closely, noting as many of the features as she could.

"It was covered in orangy-brown hair but didn't have a lot of hair on its face or its hands or abdomen. And it didn't have just a head as a lump on the shoulders [like an ape], this had more of a neck, but not much."

She surmised the ice had been created using a garden hose due to the bubbles dispersed throughout. If it had been distilled water, she pointed out, it would have been more clear. "It looked like a homemade job."

There was also a rancid smell coming from the display. The thing appeared to have been dead for a period of time before it was frozen and that was another reason Judy felt it was real. "It was definitely putrescent and you never forget that smell," she told me.

After ten minutes, Judy and the other patrons were ushered out of the trailer to make way for a new group. But that didn't stop Judy from continuing her examination. She promptly got back in line, paid another dollar, and went back inside. She soaked up every detail, trying to memorize it as much as possible.

"You could see its teeth because it had a rictus grin," she continued. "Where the lips were drawn back you could see its teeth which were not fangs; it had teeth like you and I have. And it had brown eyes with a sclera like a human. Its feet were like what they call a 'Dutch foot' on a human; they were almost square. It had real wide feet, almost as wide as they were long, and short, stubby toes. The last two toes were so short they weren't clearly separated. It also had stubby fingers too and broad hands."

Judy ended up going inside the trailer 4-5 times, which amounted to at least 30 minutes of viewing (and would cost about $40.00 in today's dollars.) It was an amazing sight that left her not only spellbound, but full of questions. She explained that two men were running the operation and were growing somewhat uncomfortable with her going in so many times. All she could learn of its origin was that it was supposedly shot at a well-known fruit tree nursery in Louisiana, Missouri. She felt certain that sometime prior to her viewing the "corpse," the nursery had offered a "bounty" for killing *something* which had been seen eating the buds from the trees and interfering with their business.[iii]

When Ms. Gustin finished the story, I considered the tantalizing connection to Momo's stomping ground. But the Momo frenzy would not take place for eight more years! Even if the story

---

iii During my research, I contacted the nursery in question (whom I will leave off the record) to inquire about such a bounty, but the owners who were alive at the time are no longer with us. I spoke to descendants of the original owners, but none could recall anything about a bounty - possibly because they were very young at the time. Ultimately, I could not verify a connection to the nursery.

of the shooting was made up, it was beyond weird that it would be set in the very same location.

As I puzzled over this strange coincidence, I considered the obvious similarity to the Minnesota Iceman case. The Iceman was a very well-known and documented exhibit which made the rounds at carnivals and fairs during the late 1960s and '70s. The exhibit was operated by carnie Frank D. Hansen and featured a similar hairy hominid frozen in a block of ice.

The saga of the Minnesota Iceman is long, winding, and full of slippery facts, but in short Hanson claimed the creature – if you will – came into his possession in 1967 when a mysterious man approached him at a sideshow and offered him the chance to display it.[85] The body, Hansen initially said, had been found by Russian seal hunters while it was floating in a block of ice along the Siberian coastline. This origin story changed several times over the years until Hansen finally claimed it had been shot while on a hunting trip in Minnesota. The exhibit was originally billed as the "Siberskoye Creature" when it was first shown in 1967, but later became more widely known as the "Minnesota Iceman."

When the exhibit showed up at a large annual fair in Chicago in 1968, it was seen by aspiring naturalist, Terry Cullen, who then brought it to the attention of well-known cryptozoologists Bernard Heuvelmans and Ivan T. Sanderson. Heuvelmans and Sanderson immediately contacted Hansen and asked for permission to view the specimen in a private setting. Hansen agreed, allowing the two cryptozoologists to examine it at his home in December 1969 while it was being stored for the winter season. It was still frozen, however.

After a thorough examination – as best one can do with a specimen under ice – both Heuvelmans and Sanderson came to the conclusion that it had once been a living creature. One reason for this was that during the examination process, a heated lamp cracked the glass cover and slightly melted a portion of the ice. The two men could smell a distinct odor of decaying flesh coming from the opening. Both men made their findings public, which included very detailed notes and drawings.

The specimen was later examined by John Napier, a primatologist for the Smithsonian Institute, who was convinced it was merely a latex fabrication. Hansen had an explanation for this, however, confessing that it was actually a substitute for the original, real corpse which he had been forced to hide. When Heuvelmans and Sanderson went public with their findings, it attracted the attention of authorities. If it were a dead body, it would be illegal to transport across state lines, which Hansen had been doing as he traveled to various fairs. Not to mention, there was a question of how the thing was killed in the first place. When local police began to question him, Hansen said he returned the original specimen to its mysterious owner and then commissioned a replica so he could continue showing the attraction.

While this sounds like a likely story from a professional carnie, Sanderson confirmed the body seen by Napier looked noticeably different than what he and Heuvelmans had inspected. Photos taken at different times over the years seem to confirm this, the mouth closed in one photo and open in another, although skeptics point out that if Hansen thawed and refroze a latex model, it might cause it to appear different from year to year.

Regardless, the mystery endures as to whether there was truly a real body being shown as the Minnesota Iceman prior to the alleged substitution. I can personally attest to the existence of the latex version since I was one of the first people to see the genuine item after it emerged from obscurity in 2013. The famous sideshow exhibit – lost from the world for at least 30 years – showed up that year on eBay and was purchased by my friend Steve Busti, owner of the Museum of the Weird in Austin, Texas. The auction included the famous gaff along with the original Minnesota Iceman freezer case and signage used for its display. Busti arranged for the items to be transported from Minnesota to Texas by way of the television show, *Shipping Wars*. I appeared in the episode along with Busti and my colleague Ken Gerhard as we treated the truck driver to an impromptu Bigfoot investigation in Fouke, Arkansas, while she was en route to the final destination in Austin.

We're driving a bit far off the Momo track now, but a brief foray into the Iceman mystery was necessary in order to evaluate whether Judy Gustin saw a version of the famed Minnesota Iceman or whether she saw something completely different. In trying to sort out the possibilities, I asked her if she was sure about the date of 1964. According to records, the famous Iceman didn't appear on the scene until 1967. Could she be confused about the date? I questioned her about this several times, but Ms. Gustin was absolutely certain of the 1964 date due to where she was living and her age at the time. Ms. Gustin is a college educated woman who comes across as very intelligent and meticulous, and even though I quizzed her to be certain, I was confident she was recalling solid facts.

And there were other details which suggested she did in fact see a different exhibit. In all its incarnations, the Minnesota Iceman is posed in a distinct position with its left arm raised over its head. Judy was positive the thing she had seen had both arms positioned down so that its hands essentially covered its crotch area. She also distinctly recalled the gunshot wound to the chest. The Iceman appeared to have a wound, but it was located on the face, not the chest. The Iceman had dark hair, while the thing she saw had lighter, reddish hair.

I spoke to Ms. Gustin on several occasions in an effort to make absolutely sure we could rule out the Minnesota specimen. In the process, her neighbor was able to show her photos of the Iceman on her smart phone. Once Judy saw these, she was certain.

"What I saw was completely different," she told me. "The thing [Iceman] in those photos looked fake to me. What I saw was a dead animal."

By that point I was convinced. But if it wasn't the Minnesota Iceman, then what was it? The Iceman hadn't been the only "missing link" type exhibit shown back in those days, but the others didn't appear until the 1970s – well after 1964. Could this one have truly come from the woods of Missouri? Was it related to Momo, whether by hoax or by real flesh? Like the rest of the case, it's a tendril of mystery that stretches into the twisting shadows of the Mississippi basin.

On the set of Shipping Wars – the "Iceman" is in the trailer.
Left to Right: John Attaway, Ken Gerhard, Chris Buntenbah,
Steve Busti, Lyle Blackburn
(Photo by Lloyd Sutton)

Chapter 4.

AFTERMATH

By mid-August 1972 things were beginning to quiet down in Louisiana. The townsfolk were still vigilant, but for several weeks no one sighted the creature or its telltale footprints. No UFOs had been seen either, following the incidents of July 30 as reported by the Shade family.

Edgar Harrison, the monster's most passionate pursuer, was also losing steam. During the commotion his home had become something of a "monster central" with a constant stream of curious visitors, pushy reporters, and a phone ringing off the hook at all hours. Since his family had left the house on July 14, he had taken a leave of absence from his job at the town waterworks and spent more than three weeks straight searching for the creature. By August he had lost weight and was both physically and mentally exhausted.

The Harrison family needed to get back to some semblance of normal life but they were reluctant to return to their house. Despite being worn out, Edgar decided to move his family to a new residence where his daughter Doris and son Terry wouldn't be reminded of their frightening experience every time they went into the backyard. The Momo craze was still reaping tourism benefits for the town, but for the Harrisons it had stolen their peace. Not only had they been uprooted from their home, but Doris and Terry had become inexorably linked to a creature which most looked upon with suspicion or humor. As a result

Edgar Harrison holding a cast of a suspected Momo footprint
(Credit: Louisiana Press-Journal)

they often suffered ridicule in addition to constant interruption by reporters and curiosity seekers. As a father, Edgar desperately wanted to prove their story, if not to himself, then to the world. But for all his time and effort, he had failed to find the perpetrator – be it man or monster – which had brought unrest to his town and family.

By August, even the footprint evidence had fallen under

the weight of scrutiny. Hayden Hewes of Oklahoma had made plaster casts of two of the suspected footprints and taken them back home to be examined by Lawrence Curtis, director of the Oklahoma City Zoo. In a statement to reporters Curtis admitted it was possible "an unknown species of animal could be living in the Missouri forests," however, he felt the tracks themselves had been hoaxed.[86]

Ironically, Curtis had previous experience with alleged "monster tracks" due to his involvement with Oklahoma's notorious Abominable Chicken Man case. In December 1970, a farmer near the small town of Reno discovered several primate-like handprints on a chicken coop whose door had literally been ripped from its hinges and thrown to the ground. When the state game warden was summoned to the scene, he decided to send the door to Curtis for examination. Curtis agreed the handprints appeared "to be like those of a primate," yet very unusual. "It resembles a gorilla," he told reporters at the time, "but it's more like a man."[87] Curtis wasn't alone in his opinion, as other mammologists who examined the handprints felt they were definitely made by some type of primate. In the case of the Momo footprints, however, Curtis felt differently. "On the basis of our examination," Curtis said, "we think they [the Momo footprints] are fakes."[88]

Other alleged Momo evidence didn't even receive the benefit of proper examination. Harrison had also given Hewes two strands of suspected Momo hair, which were supposed to be sent to the prominent cryptozoologist, Ivan Sanderson, who was also a qualified zoologist. Apparently, Sanderson never received them.[89]

The Missouri Department of Conservation clung to the belief that if people had seen and heard strange things in the area, then a bear was likely to blame, even though bears were not known to inhabit the area. According to the Conservation Department at the time, bears were extremely rare in Missouri outside the deep woods of the southern Ozarks. Although much of the state has sufficient wooded hills, it was not preferable to bears due to a lack of berries and a winter season that was often too warm. This reduced their hibernation period and forced them to scavenge the woods when food was scarce.[90]

"In stacking up the territorial requirements, diversity and abundance of fruiting trees and shrubs needed [for bears], as well as range undisturbed by humans," said Frank Sampson, Missouri's game biologist, "there is little doubt that what Missouri has to offer is, at the very least, highly dubious in supporting anything like a huntable population."[91]

That being said, the Department of Conservation noted that more bears had been drifting up from Arkansas into Missouri, and perhaps a few of these individuals traveled north along the river for a visit to Louisiana.

The department cited an incident from Friday June 28, 1972 in which a woman reportedly saw a small, black bear near the foot of Marzolf Hill. That day Opal Anderson, along with her husband, were in town visiting her mother, Mrs. Mary Pearl, who lived on Dougherty-Pike Road. At around 7:30 p.m. they were sitting inside the house when Mrs. Pearl's dog began making a "terrible racket" outside.[92] They didn't pay much attention at first, but when the dog continued to bark, Opal went into the backyard to have a look.

Opal told a reporter from the *Louisiana Press-Journal* that once she entered the yard, she walked in the direction where the dog seemed to be pointing and barking. The yard extended for about 60 feet from the house to the Town Branch Creek which runs along the base of Marzolf Hill. Once she got to the creek, she looked over a ledge. Down below, she saw what appeared to be a "little bitty bear."

"When I called to the rest of the family to come quick, the bear loped off," Opal said. Her husband, who ran out first, managed to get a glimpse of it as it "vanished into the weeds." He jumped down and tried to head it off before it could get away, but it ran deeper into the heavy undergrowth and was gone. Upon further inspection, they found a thin trail through the brush where something had been traveling back and forth.

State conservation officer, Gus Artus, said he was made aware of the report and on Saturday morning spent two hours searching for the bear behind the Anderson's home. He found no sign of it, but noted "it would be easy to miss a bear in the heavy undergrowth, and the ground was too dry and gravelly to leave tracks."[93]

The bear could've been responsible for some unusual sounds, but with its small size, it could hardly be mistaken for a tall, upright creature covered in long hair. This would have required a much larger, shaggier bear with a talent for walking on two legs. Conflicting views such as this left Momo to skulk in a fog of speculation as August wrapped up without so much as an odoriferous whiff.

It's Back!?

Just when residents were beginning to breathe a sigh of relief, a rumor that Momo had been seen again quickly spread around Louisiana. According to the story, the creature had been hit by a truck as it dashed across Highway 79 south of town. The driver, they said, reported the incident to police but the police refused to investigate the matter.

"It looked to me like a man," James Davis said, while clarifying the facts with a reporter from the *Press-Journal* on September 11. He had seen something odd near his home on Highway 79, but it didn't appear to be covered in hair.

According to Davis, on the night of September 8, he had driven his car to a local nursing home to pick up his wife from work. On the drive back they had just passed over the Noix Creek bridge on Highway 79 and were within about 200 feet of their house, when Davis saw what appeared to be the silhouette of a large man standing near his truck, which was parked outside.

"I couldn't tell whether he was facing me or was looking away," Davis explained. As the Davises approached in the car, the figure "stepped away from the truck and stood spraddle-legged on the east side of the highway." It then turned and ran into a nearby driveway.

Davis, unsure about what he was seeing and whether it may have been an intruder, drove past his house before turning around further down the road. He then returned and parked outside his house.

Davis's son – who was home at the time – had heard some kind of noise and was already outside the house investigating. Davis and his son then proceeded to search around the house and in the brush behind it for anything they could find. They also searched an abandoned house near the property.

During the search, Davis went to his neighbor's house to borrow a better flashlight. At that time he asked the neighbor to call the police. Upon returning to his own house, Davis and his son noticed the side-view mirror on their truck was dented and broken. They also saw a "gray stain" on the side of the truck and a similar stain below the mirror. Whatever the substance was, it appeared to have dripped down causing some discoloration.

The next morning, Davis found a large, half-eaten pear on the opposite side of Highway 79. Upon comparing it to the dent in the truck's mirror housing, Davis felt the pear may have been thrown at the car, thus causing the damage and perhaps producing the noise his son heard.

When another local resident, George Minor, came by to have a look, he found "what seemed to be an unusual footprint in the sand by the truck." It was at the exact spot where Davis had seen the "large man." Minor suggested it might be "similar to the tracks reportedly found earlier when the 'Mo-Mo' incident was at its height." Talk of this incident undoubtedly started the rumor which was then distorted by a few gossipy twists.

Whether Davis saw a man or something else, the shadowy

sighting was a reminder that the locals could not easily forget the specter of the creature which haunted them. Whenever someone drove down a dark street or strolled through a wooded area, they couldn't help but wonder if it was still out there, perhaps watching them. People had their theories but nothing had been officially resolved. Anything was still possible.

As fall progressed, however, no additional incidents were reported. Tourists were still meandering into town but it was beginning to look as though Momo had completely dropped from the radar, leaving the town of Louisiana with both newfound fame and a heck of a lingering mystery. One that perhaps was not over.

Lingering Traces

As it is with so many of these highly publicized "monster cases," the media is quick to cover the stories or reprint the articles, but if no reasonable conclusion is found within a month or so, they tend to drop it and move on. It's true that the majority of strange incidents did take place during July of 1972, and that's where you'll find the major news coverage, but there were residual incidents that either went unreported or were never made public at the time. This progression makes it hard to define any sort of clear-cut end to the matter. If it were an animal, did it simply move on? If it were a hoax, did the perpetrator or perpetrators simply quit the antics? Or had it been one big hallucination for an entire community?

On October 29, 1972, just 30 miles northeast of Louisiana across the river, John Roman and his wife were in the woods near Chestline, Illinois, when he came face-to-face with something he'll never forget. It was Sunday morning and they were packing up their tent after a long weekend of camping. At one point, Roman decided to take a smoke break.

"I went down a path and sat on a rock and smoked a cigarette," Roman told investigator Stan Courtney in an interview.[94] "I heard a sound behind me [so] I turned around and about I would say twenty feet, maybe a little further, standing downslope, was what I thought initially was a very large man in a fur get-up."

Roman was surprised to see anyone since they were the only campers in the area at the time. Surprise quickly turned to alarm, however, when he realized it wasn't a man in a fur suit. It appeared to be some kind of animal with a human appearance.

"[It] was about seven-feet-tall, maybe taller, and we locked eyes for just a matter of a few seconds," he told Courtney. "It was standing there... and its left hand was holding onto a tree."

Roman could clearly see its body was covered in hair. The color varied in shades of brown and dark-brown to gray. Overall it was very bulky with wide shoulders. He could only see it from about the waist up because it was standing on the downward side of the slope. Unlike most witnesses in the Momo case, he had a very clear view of its facial features.

"The face looked more human than ape," Roman explained. "[It's] the only thing I can remember in detail to this day. The nose was large and flat, but did not have turned up nostrils like a gorilla. Its teeth were really big and really yellow [and] it had a heavy brow. It looked like a real ugly human."

Whatever it was, Roman got the feeling the thing was just as startled to see him as he was to see it. Its eyes darted back and forth, as if it were contemplating what to do. "Then it rounded the tree and took off down the slope of a gully and I took off up the path running like crazy," Roman said. "I was scared, I was really scared."

When Roman got back to camp and told his wife what he'd seen, she was skeptical, although she could not deny the fear in his eyes. In 1972, he and his wife had yet to hear of Bigfoot or even the recent Momo sightings in nearby Missouri. Only later did he learn of the strange similarities to both Bigfoot and to what was being seen in the town of Louisiana. At the time the incident just seemed so crazy and Roman's wife was adamant that he tell no one about what he'd seen. She didn't want to face the ridicule which would have surely come from such a story. They had no idea they were not the only ones facing this dilemma.

The following spring another strange incident occurred back in Momo's prime stomping ground. According to the witness – who was young at the time – in April 1973 his family was picking wild mushrooms in a deep hollow on the outskirts of Louisiana when they got wind of a horrible smell.[95] His mom and aunt couldn't identify a reasonable source for the smell, so they became spooked and decided to head back to the car. As locals they were acutely aware of the Momo story and knew its connection with bad odors.

They proceeded to drive to the witness' grandparents' house nearby, but found no one home. As they were about to drive back out, they heard a very loud and unusual scream coming from the area where they experienced the smell. The witness' mother suggested it might be a panther, although she seemed uncertain. As such, they quickly left the area.

After relaying the story to the grandmother, she said she'd also smelled the strange odor while out picking blackberries and, perhaps, had even seen the infamous beast. One night she was looking out her backdoor when she saw "what appeared to be two red glowing eyes peering back at her."[96] Two other members of the family claimed they'd also seen something that looked like a "7-8 foot tall, hairy creature standing on its hind legs staring at them." The neighbors had also seen the thing and ran outside to get a better look. Whatever it was fled into the woods, but not without leaving footprints in a spot of fresh mud. The prints were approximately 15 inches long.

In the summer of 1974, two men encountered the same sort of putrid odor while on the Mississippi River Road in nearby Calhoun County, Illinois. In an interview with Stan Courtney, one of the witnesses said he and his friend were riding along the road at 10:00 p.m. when they needed to stop and "relieve themselves."[97] As they opened the car doors they were overcome with a terrible stench, which he described as "the worst odor we had ever smelled."

The young men walked to the back of the car to do their business. When they got there, they heard what sounded like breathing. "I looked toward the breathing sound up a 5-foot embankment," the witness said. "Standing still, next to a fence post was a dark, tall wide figure facing me."

The figure was approximately 20 feet away, and judging by the size of the fence post, it was at least seven feet tall. It was very bulky and dark in color which made the witness suspect it was not a person. To him, it seemed to be some type of animal.

The men were so frightened, they immediately jumped back in the car and sped off. They were so shaken, they rode in silence for at least 10 miles before discussing what they'd seen. They both agreed it was not something they wanted to tell others about. And so it was years before the incident became public.

It's hard to say whether these Illinois incidents were related to Momo, but they were certainly within the same region and fit the same sort of profile with their descriptions and associated odors. As for Pike County itself, there seems to be one last occurrence of something mysterious before it finally faded away. During my research I spoke to Joanna Minor who told me her grandfather had seen something fitting the description of Momo around 1974. Minor said her grandparents lived near Louisiana, close to the river. They were of course familiar with the Momo story, but considered it to be total nonsense. That presumption would be challenged one morning as her grandfather drove to work in the early hours. As he neared Battle Creek, he noticed a large, human-like figure come from the woods and move towards the edge of the road some distance ahead. The sun was just beginning to peek above the horizon and he had his headlamps on, so visibility was fairly good. As he got closer, whatever it was darted across the road with long, quick strides. It appeared to be covered in dark hair, and was tall and ape-like, yet stayed upright on two feet the entire time.

Shocked, her grandfather immediately slowed the vehicle and watched as the thing jumped a ditch and ran into the trees beyond. It looked agile, giving him the impression it was some kind of animal as opposed to a person dressed in a clunky costume. The location was rather desolate and creepy in the early morning hours, so he quickly sped up and left the area.

Whether this was the last time someone saw something strange in Pike County, we may never know. However, Momo never left the town of Louisiana.

Rise of an Icon

In the years to follow, Momo would become an inseparable part of Louisiana town history, if not a mainstay of Missouri folklore. During the original craze, local disc jockey Bill Whyte recorded a tongue-in-cheek song called "Momo the Missouri Monster" for KPCR Radio out of nearby Bowling Green. The song, written by Joe Lewis and studio owner Paul Salois, was catchy and fun which helped to fuel the Momo frenzy and ensure its endurance.

A local bowling team, the Zephyr Monsters, adopted Momo as their mascot. Their t-shirts depicted a hairy beast with a bowling ball. At Halloween, kids began to dress up in homemade Momo costumes while a few adults constructed huge Momo props to complement their outdoor Halloween decorations.

As a town, Louisiana was not shy to embrace the lighthearted side of their local monster either. For a period of several years afterwards, they hosted a Momo Days Festival in which residents not only enjoyed fair-type activities, but dressed in matted wigs to celebrate what had become their most famous resident.

A short distance away in St. Louis, the popular amuse-

Kids dressed as "Momo" - Halloween 1972
(Credit: Louisiana Press-Journal)

ment park, Six Flags Over Mid-America, capitalized on Momo's fame by adding a "MoMo the Monster" ride in 1973. The ride was representative of Momo only in name, however, as it looked more like a tentacled sea creature than a hairy beast. Its tentacle-like arms spun in one direction while passenger buckets swayed back and forth. Halfway through the ride the arms stopped and the ride would spin the opposite direction. MoMo the Monster remained a popular ride until it was eventually replaced by another in 1994.[98]

Newspaper coverage of Momo ceased in 1972, although subsequent articles in prominent paranormal publications – such as *FATE* magazine – continued to spread the story to a worldwide audience. Even though other towns had experienced similar monster outbreaks at the same time (some of which were mentioned earlier), it was Momo who had the appeal and staying power to become an icon of both Missouri legend and cryptozoology alike. The fact that several artistic renderings had appeared along with the stories undoubtedly helped, while the mental image of a hair-covered beast with a large head and a dog in its grasp make it hard to forget.

The lasting impression was underscored by various attempts to recreate a Momo scare in their own town. A few years later, some kids in Joplin, Missouri, got ahold of a $12 gorilla suit and began jumping out at residents at night. Reporters naturally made references to Momo, conjecturing that perhaps the creature had relocated. It wasn't long before the police figured out it was a prank, however, and put an end to the affair. Police told reporters they were amazed the kids hadn't been shot. As in the Momo case, panic-stricken locals quickly took to the woods with guns.[99]

MoMo the Monster ride at Six Flags Over Mid-America
(Credit: St. Louis Post-Dispatch)

MOMO: THE STRANGE CASE OF THE MISSOURI MONSTER

Over the years, Momo's relationship to the study of UFOs has remained tentative, with the creature occasionally being mentioned in connection with the UFO activity in the area. As a Bigfoot story, the tale of Momo has become a genuine classic among those beyond Bigfoot's traditional stomping ground of the Pacific Northwest. In terms of Midwest and Southern Sasquatch type creatures, Momo's notoriety is perhaps only eclipsed by Arkansas' Boggy Creek Monster which was the subject of the popular 1972 film, *The Legend of Boggy Creek*. The film's massive success along with the aggressive and dramatic nature of the Boggy Creek encounters helped to ensure its longevity. Yet, even without a cinematic vehicle, Momo has managed to maintain icon status within American monster lore.

Momo's mark is still evident today. Every few years the story is revisited by local news journalists as well as writers from around the country who cover strange legends and cryptid reports (myself included). A search for Momo on the inter-webs results in numerous hits – from newspaper articles to blogs to rehashed versions of the (mostly incomplete) story. Television shows, such as *Monsters and Mysteries in America*, have also delved into Momo's hairy history as they explored various topics of cryptozoology.

Momo has even entered the modern pop culture market in the form of action figures, artwork, and trading cards. The most notable of these products is an action figure produced by Todd Broadwater's Legendary Toys. The now-defunct company was a small, independent affair which produced a limited number of stylized cryptid figures backed by a crowd-funding campaign. The Momo figure stands 5.5 inches tall and features the trademark hair-covered face and blood-splattered fur. It was packaged in a cardboard box made to look like a wooden crate and released in a very small quantity in 2014.

As someone who is known for researching these type cases, I'm often asked what I think about Momo, or... *dramatic pause...*

Momo action figure by Legendary Toys
(Credit: Todd Broadwater)

if I'm going to 'write a book about it?' And I can't say I'm surprised. It's certainly a standout among real-life monster tales, and with the periphery phenomenon, it's a story that continues to draw interest from a variety of angles.

But no matter which facet of the Momo case draws the interest, the road of research inevitably leads to one big question: What was – or is – Momo? Are we dealing with a rogue bear, an unknown primate, an alien, or simply a well-played hoax? Over the years, more information has ebbed from the hills and hollows of Louisiana which will either answer these very questions or add yet another layer of Mississippi silt to this classic Missouri mystery.

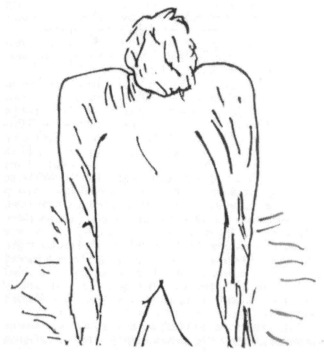

Edgar Harrison's drawing of Momo as directed by Doris and Terry Harrison (Credit: Flying Saucer Review)

Chapter 5.

NATURE OF THE BEAST

From the moment the Missouri Monster story was introduced to the public, the true nature of the "beast" was hotly debated. Locals in the town of Louisiana had their own theories, while the rest of the world conjectured from afar. Was the creature some type of unknown primate? Was it simply a bear? Did it come from one of the UFOs sighted in the area? Could it have been a hoax perpetrated by teenagers? Or was the whole thing simply a mass hallucination fed by fears and media interest?

While each theory has its own merits, there's certainly no reason to believe the whole thing was the result of mass hallucination. There were just too many sightings by credible individuals, some occurring in full daylight. The reports by the Harrison kids and the women who were picnicking are the best examples. Their proximity to the subject, their descriptions, and their subsequent actions are simply too palpable for it to have been a figment of imagination. Even if the rest of the sightings are eliminated, these two incidents alone are enough to rule out a theory of mass hallucination, as defined by the common interpretation of 'hallucination.'

Outright fabrication can seemingly be ruled out as well. Sure, kids have active imaginations, but the fear and trauma exhibited by the Harrison kids was apparent to all who spoke to them at the time. Even after years of scrutiny, Doris Harrison still stands behind what she saw that day in 1972. During my research

I had the good fortune of speaking with her. Her health has declined considerably, but she was still willing to share her thoughts, insights, and even direct me to some of the pertinent locations where events had occurred.

"I don't know what it was, *but I saw it*," Doris told me. I could tell by the emphasis in her words she was accustomed to defending her story. "It was big and hairy. I couldn't see its face, but it was there. It was so ratty looking."

Even before talking to her, I already knew her story wasn't fabricated. Speaking to her merely reinforced my postulation. I can't say what the Harrison kids saw, but it certainly wasn't an illusion or something they made up for fun.

Doris, who later married her boyfriend Richard Bliss, noted that police *did* take the matter seriously, and so did her father and Richard. It was not something most locals took lightly either. She felt they tried their best to hunt down, or at least find out what she and her brothers had seen. Even so, Doris was subject to ridicule and harassment at the time, and has never really been free from the reminders or folks like myself asking her to recount the story. "It happened in July which is around my birthday," she said. "So every year it starts up."

In our conversation she made a point to clarify facts about the environment around their old house where the thing was seen and heard. "People always talk about it like it was in our *backyard*," she explained, "but it wasn't a backyard, it was woods. There were woods right there behind our house." The *Monsters and Mysteries in America* episode which featured the Momo story made it appear as if some of the events took place at a campground. "They made it look like we were having a campfire up there, like it was at a campsite. But we weren't camping," she clarified.

Doris also told me about the noises coming from the woods. "When it hollered that night [after the church meeting], it was the most horrible sound I'd ever heard. It would just chill through your body. We'd had a prayer meeting that night and everybody had left. My dad was just sitting outside with his guitar and mom and I were cleaning up with my brothers and sisters. The next thing you know, that thing let out a hell of a holler. My husband was there – my boyfriend at the time – and we just all started toward the car. My little sister says she remembers Richard grabbing her and tossing her in the car by her pants. We all took off with dad hollering 'it's coming off the hill!' When I think about it now it's kind of funny the way it happened. But back then it wasn't funny; it was scary."

In the years that followed, Doris and Richard enjoyed a long, happy life still residing in Louisiana beneath the looming shadow of Marzolf Hill. Richard has since passed away, but throughout the years he stood behind what he and the family experienced. It was something they could never escape.

I asked if her younger brother, Terry, still recalled the incident and if he ever spoke about it. "He doesn't like to talk about it," she said, "I think it messed with him when he was little."

That was certainly understandable. No matter what it was, it must have been an extremely frightening experience for an eight-year-old. It was frightening enough for Doris and she was fourteen. I knew she was weary of talking about the matter, especially under the circumstances of her declining health. I told her I appreciated her taking the time to speak about something that, to her, is a thing of the past; something that she probably wished never happened. But it did, and after talking to her, I had no doubt that she and her brothers saw something that day, whether it be man or beast. It was no fabrication.

When it comes to the case of the two women, Joan Mills and Mary Ryan, fabrication also seems highly unlikely. They reported their story to the state police with no pretense of fame, glory, or riches. The act of reporting it was a testament to the truth, given the possible ridicule they could face if the story did go public. There's simply no good reason why these women would make up such a story and then report it to authorities. There can only be one explanation… like the Harrisons, they saw *something*.

Aside from these two major incidents, there were other sightings that support the notion of something tangible lurking in the area. The incident in which two fishermen saw something human-like and covered in hair wading in the Cuivre River is one such example. If their estimate of being a mere 150 feet from the thing is accurate, it's hard to imagine they would mistake it for a swimmer, hunter, "hippie," or any other type of person.

There were, of course, a handful of nighttime sightings, long-distance glimpses, and after-the-fact claims reported, but even if these are chalked up to error, we're left with enough to conclude people were indeed seeing something that was most likely physical and altogether unusual. And that's not the totality of sightings either, since some were kept off the record. When asked about it at the time, assistant police chief Jerry Floyd stated: "In all fairness, we have had other people say they've seen this thing. Most at a distance of about 20 feet and at night. Some good, reliable citizens."[100]

Given these observations, we can assume with a great degree of certainty that people did in fact see something that was truly there. The question then remains, what was it?

Bear-ly There

As mentioned previously, the Missouri Department of Conservation believed a bear was responsible for the Momo scare. Chief of Police, Shelby Ward, entertained the idea as well, but seemed to be more in favor of a hoax or unexplainable cause. Either way, it seems unlikely a bear could be at fault.

First, the key descriptions do not fit the anatomy of a bear. In the case of the two women who were picnicking, the subject came within a few feet of them as it stood outside their car window. If it were a bear, they could have easily recognized it as such. Instead, they described it in terms of a "hairy human" or "ape." It's hard to believe at that close of a range they couldn't have identified a bear or even a person in a costume.

Other witnesses were also adamant that it was much more "man-like" with body hair and hair covering much of its face. Doris assured me it was no bear. No one saw the thing drop to all fours either. In every single case, the witnesses said it was standing and walking on two legs. Bears can and do utilize bipedality, but not at length and not with such consistency.

This is not to say there weren't sightings of bears. Opal Anderson and her husband most certainly saw a small black bear on July 28. But it was just that... a small bear. It did not walk upright nor was it covered in long, shaggy hair. It may have been a juvenile from a family, but even so, a mama bear would not have a mat of long hair or a pumpkin-shaped head.

The two boys who saw a hairy animal on Marzolf Hill on July 18 told police it had a foul stench and resembled a bear, but did not say it *was* a bear. Ernest Shade and the other boys who saw something swimming across the Salt River as they were fishing on August 4 believed the animal could have been a bear, but weren't sure. Its head was "bigger than a human head" and it had what appeared to be shoulders, but there was no way to confirm whether it was a bear, a monster, or anything else.

The fact there was at least one confirmed sighting of a bear simply reinforces the notion that the area could support large wildlife. The region might not contain the vast forestry of the Ozarks, but it was still rural and rugged enough to host a bear, if not other things.

Beastly Biped

The subject reported in this case most resembles the description of a Bigfoot, and this is perhaps the most popular theory that's been offered as an explanation. As we've seen, there's a significant history of ape-like creature sightings in Missouri and the surrounding states, so it's only natural that Momo is thought to be one such creature.

To conjecture whether Momo is some type of a Bigfoot is to ask the more general question of whether Bigfoot creatures actually exist in North America at all? Without irrefutable proof this is a topic still under debate. However, there have been plenty of credible sightings and some compelling evidence in the form of hair and footprints which suggest that perhaps these creatures are real. Their uncanny ability to remain elusive may be perplexing, but the fact that we don't have a body isn't enough to dismiss the entire Bigfoot case out of hand. Just ask anyone who's had a sighting and they'll tell you.

The circumstances of the Momo encounters are consistent with those of Bigfoot, in that the sightings are somewhat brief and located within areas of woods and sufficient water supply. The creature too, like Bigfoot, is described as being large, covered in hair with ape-like features, and standing or walking upright on two legs. The only caveats are the odd, pumpkin-shaped head (reported by some) and the three-toed tracks. These traits are more unusual, yet still don't exclude Momo's membership within the Bigfoot category. While the large head is not typical of Bigfoot descriptions, their alleged characteristics do vary from witness to witness and by location. The creatures seen in the northern part of the country can often differ from those in the southern regions, which suggests there is perhaps more than one species or adaptations which have occurred in some particular environments, not to mention possible deformities or genetic aberrations.

The same can be said of the three-toed tracks, if they are indeed footprints of the subject. While the majority of Bigfoot tracks exhibit five toes, there have been a number of suspected footprints which only have three. The majority of these three-toed variety have been found in the southern parts of the United States – such as those associated with the famous Boggy Creek Monster – but not all of them. In the case of the Pennsylvania outbreak where hairy creatures were spotted in the same time frame as Momo, some of the tracks investigators found also had three toes.

This rather odd trait adds yet another level of complexity to the Bigfoot case in general, since all hominoids (i.e., anthropoid apes and human beings) have five toes. Three toes is not only uncharacteristic, it defies physical logic in that it would be difficult for a creature standing seven-feet-tall and weighing in excess of 400 pounds to maintain proper balance and agility with this type of foot. As upright-walking hominoids, we have five toes for a reason. It's simply the best construction for efficient and effective motility.

But alas, there have been a number of theories offered to explain the three-toed anomaly. Among these is the possibility of genetic deformity. If these creatures do exist, they would surely be limited to small populations in which inbreeding may occur. A common result of inbreeding is congenital deformations of the foot and hand which manifest as missing digits.

Injury could also explain the anomaly. Walking barefoot in muddy waters and deep woods has its risks and may result in the loss of a few digits, if for example, the subject stepped on something sharp or had a run-in with an alligator who snipped himself a snack.

It's also possible the footprints were nothing more than hoaxes fueled by the moment and completely unrelated to the alleged creature at all. This type of scenario can be found in other cases such as the Bishopville Lizard Man, where credible sightings did occur while at the same time some kids tried to add their own stamp to the media frenzy by faking footprints. In the case of Momo, similar revelations have surfaced which we will address shortly.

If Momo were a Bigfoot, then presumably the sightings would only end if the creature died or moved on. While it would be impossible to know whether the creature died (outside of finding the remains), the possibility of moving on seems logical considering these events took place along a waterway. Cases where a concentrated outbreak of Bigfoot sightings occur along rivers and creeks can be brief, as if the creature or creatures were merely moving through or traveling up and down a certain stretch of water. In some of these cases, additional outbreaks will occur at points along the waterway during the same time period or perhaps at a later date. As we've seen, there had been strange encounters reported along that stretch of the Mississippi River corridor in the past, and even during the Momo frenzy when people reported a similar entity along the banks of the Cuivre River south of Louisiana. These type of scattered sightings along a river corridor are consistent with Bigfoot cases, especially in the Southern states where waterways connect areas of discontiguous forestry.

The main wave of Momo sightings happened in a concentrated period of the early 1970s, however, there have been additional reports logged across Missouri in the years since. In a letter to Bobbie Short, moderator of the Bigfoot Encounters website, Mark Richardson claims he saw a "Momo" along a railroad in St. Peters, Missouri, in the late 1970s.[101] He was 20 years old at the time and he and a friend were hanging around the old railroad bridge which crosses Dardenne Creek, a tributary of the Missouri River. As they were climbing on the bridge at different locations, Richardson noticed some shadowy movement in the trees but didn't think too much of it at the moment. Later, as his friend was answering the call of nature at the opposite end of the bridge, something emerged from the woods, jumped on the railroad timbers and tried to grab him!

Richardson watched in horror as his friend jumped back and scrambled away. According to Richardson: "The creature was approximately 8 to 9 feet tall" with "very long and matted hair on [its] whole body." It's hair color was "very dark brown" and its eyes were barely visible through the hair. It was massive with a shoulder span of approximately five feet. It also had a "very short neck" and "its arms were long as the hands hung past the knees." The body shape, he said "looked like the classic Bigfoot pictures, except the arms were longer and the hands were different." The hands appeared to have only three fingers.

Richardson's friend managed to evade the creature and both young men fled as fast as they could from the area. The creature let out a "scream like a panther" which fueled their pell-mell escape even more.

Richardson said they finally got up the nerve to return to the bridge at a later date. As they were investigating the area, they found some impressions which appeared to be handprints. "We saw the imprints of the fingers and the nails in the soft mud of the creek banks," he explained. "The odd part was we never found a footprint. I say these were handprints only because they wouldn't support a creature of this size. All three fingers were approximately 1.5 inch in diameter and approximately 8-inches long. I assume it walked mainly in the water, [in order] to leave as few tracks as possible."

The creature also had a foul, rotten odor which they smelled whenever it was seen or when they believed it was creeping around the area. "It moved very quiet in the creek and the woods for an animal of this size," he noted.

The creature was reportedly seen several times, not only by Richardson and his friend, but by others. "We [saw] it maybe 4 to 5 times in a short period of time," Richardson said. "I guess it went to a different location on the creek. I have told many people of this sighting over the years and no one believes it."

Around 1977, Shawn Brower saw what appeared to be a large, hairy bipedal creature near Table Rock Lake in Southwest Missouri. Brower told me he was young at the time and was visiting his grandparents' house located on Joe Bald Road. One afternoon he was playing in their backyard by himself when he looked up at a large hill which stood to the east. At the top was a clearing with a rocky area and a fallen tree.

"As I was looking up there I saw something walk across

the clearing," Brower explained. "It was a large, man-shaped being that looked like it was covered in fur and much taller than any man I had ever seen."

The strange entity walked across the clearing in full view before it disappeared back into the woods. Brower said he was so frightened by what he saw that he hid underneath a picnic table until his grandmother eventually came out and found him. When he told her what he'd seen, she dismissed it as childhood fantasy. However, Brower can still remember the incident vividly and believes what he saw was not human.

A mere 20 miles west, across the woods and waterways of the southwest segment of the Mark Twain National Forest, Michael Rocco saw something similar in 1997. After having met Rocco in person during one of my trips to the Missouri-Arkansas area, he submitted a detailed account. In the account, Rocco explained that he and his brother, Mark, were camping in the Roaring River State Park on the night of July 27. At around 2:00 a.m., they were sitting around a dying campfire talking and listening to music when Rocco noticed a large, dark shape moving along the deserted park road about thirty feet away. He first thought it was a person walking on the road, although it was very late for anyone to be taking a stroll. As the figure drew nearer, however, he changed his mind. It looked human-like, but its shape and movements were inexplicably different.

"As it got closer, I realized that I was seeing something very extraordinary," Rocco said. "I could see that it was definitely an upright creature on two legs. There was something different about the gait and its arm movement."

Darkness surrounded their campsite, but there was a mercury flood-lamp mounted on a pole part way up a nearby hill. It illuminated the scene well enough for Rocco to get a good, silhouette view of the entity.

"It was a large creature that I estimate around seven to eight feet tall," Rocco recalled. "Its arms were very muscular... the

chest was massive. The head appeared to have long straight hair…
and [it] had a protruding forehead… and jutting lantern jaw."

Michael quickly nudged his brother and told him to look
up. When he did, Mark caught a glimpse of the thing as it moved
behind their tent and disappeared into the woods beyond. Seconds later, Mark gasped something to the effect of 'what the hell
was that!?'

The brothers remained frozen for a few seconds as they
tried to rationalize what they had just seen. Rocco said his own
thoughts raced with "excitement and fear." He wanted to pursue
the creature, but was hesitant since he was unsure what might be
waiting out there in the dark. In the end, the brothers decided it
might be best to leave it alone.

"I don't know if this was a Sasquatch or a primitive man,
or perhaps something else," Rocco concluded. He regrets not pur-

*The area of Roaring River where Michael Rocco
and his brother saw the mysterious figure
(Photo by Michael Rocco)*

suing it, but in the moment, an encounter like that can be understandably startling.

Even in Pike County itself, there have been subsequent incidents eerily reminiscent of the Momo affair. In 1991, two men said they were camping near Louisiana when one of them saw something which fit the description of Momo.[102] It was early spring and storms were threatening the skies. As they were driving in, they noticed the wildlife seemed unusually active, perhaps due to the imminent rain. Several deer scampered across the road and one nearly jumped onto the hood of their jeep, which they found rather odd.

Despite the strange atmosphere and potential storm, the men decided they would brave it out and continue on to the camp. Once there, one of the men used an ATV to scout for firewood along the woods at the back of the farm. As he was driving, he began to smell a horrible odor. A few seconds later he was startled by a shocking sight.

"I looked to my left and in the creek I saw a creature that looked like a large ape or bear," he said. It was crouched in the creek staring at him. He stopped the ATV and peered at the thing.

"It looked right into my eyes," he explained. "We stared at each other for what seemed like forever but it was probably about 30 seconds, then it turned its head and from a squatting position, jumped up an eight-foot bank and ran in the other direction."

The man raced the ATV back to the campsite where he told his friend what he'd seen. After calming down, they grabbed their guns and headed back down to the creek to see if they could see it again. "When we arrived at the spot it was getting dark and we didn't want to stay around after dark," he admitted. "[So] we returned to where I saw the creature in the morning to look for footprints, but the creeks were flooded from the storm and we found no evidence."

The camp was located at the back of the family's farm

which had three creeks running through it, along with some hilly terrain and a small cave. "It's about five miles from the farm to Louisiana, Missouri, with thick forest and little population separating the two," he noted.

The mention of the cave is interesting, and another aspect of the Bigfoot conversation since many have theorized that if these creatures do exist in that part of the country, they may utilize caves as a means of concealment and survival. Missouri in particular is known for its network of caves, and is often referred to as "The Cave State" by spelunking aficionados.

On the whole, Missouri has more than 7,300 documented caves with perhaps many more yet to be discovered. Most of these are "wild caves," with only 20 being open to the public as "show caves."[103] The abundance of caves in this region can be attributed to Missouri's rich deposits of dolomite and limestone. Since these type of rocks can be dissolved by water, natural drainage results in the formation of numerous springs and caves. These cavities are often connected to the rivers and streams as they provide corridors of movement for the water network.

While most of Missouri's caves are found south of the Missouri River in the Ozarks, there are still plenty within the state's Northeast Karst Region, an area which encompasses Pike County. The most prominent and famous caves in this region are the Cameron Cave and Mark Twain Cave near Hannibal. These are classified as "maze caves" due to their unique karst features and numerous winding passages. The Mark Twain Cave – originally known as McDougal's Cave – is particularly vast, and at the time when author Mark Twain resided in the area, it was still largely unexplored.

Aside from these well-known caves, there's hundreds of other caves and sinkholes, only some of which have been documented. According to Jeff Crews, a geologist with the Department of Natural Resources' division of Geology and Land Survey: "Only four of the 226 known caves in the northeast region have been explored for more than a mile in length. Most of the caves lie on the flanks of the Lincoln Fold that parallels the Mississippi River. Also in the hills and hollers close by are other caves just as complex with parts still unexplored by man."[104] That, it seems, leaves a lot of places for anything to hide.

During my research into the Momo case, I came across an interesting story involving a cave on the outskirts of the town of Louisiana. According to my colleague, Jerry Hestand, a local history buff informed him that a "monkey skull" had supposedly been found inside it years ago. The cave, in this case, is essentially an underground tunnel which has an entrance at both ends. About halfway through the formation, there's a small cavern where the skull was supposedly located. Of course no official verification or examination of the skull was ever conducted, so it's hard to say whether it was indeed that of a primate. But regardless, it was something the locals apparently knew of and talked about. In fact, the cave was often called Monkey Cave due to the bizarre discovery. Unfortunately we couldn't run down any further details about the skull, so it merely remains an interesting footnote to both the Momo case and the possible use of caves by unexpected or unknown animals.

Scattered reports have continued to come in from the area over the years. As recently as 2007, a man hunting on the Illinois-side of Pike County saw something that can only be described as a Bigfoot. In an interview with Stan Courtney, the witness said he went deer hunting on November 16.[105] He was in his tree stand very early in the morning, around 6:20 a.m., when he heard footsteps coming from a pasture off to his right. Believing it was another hunter headed for a nearby ground blind, the witness stood up to see who it was. Instead of a hunter, however, he was shocked to see a large, hairy animal walking upright with huge strides. It was less than 20 yards away.

"I would estimate it to be 6 to 7 feet tall," he said. "[It was] walking very quickly like it knew where it was going."

The hunter was confident the figure was not a man. It wasn't wearing the characteristic blaze-orange or any other type of clothing. Its muscular body was covered in dark, rusty-brown hair and it had long arms, broad shoulders, and relatively no neck. The hunter could not make out any facial features since the creature never looked towards him. It simply walked on, eventually out of sight.

Not surprisingly, the hunter was both startled and frightened by what he saw. In his own words: "I was freaked out." And who could blame him? The sight of something like that in the modern world would certainly be unsettling, if not life-changing as any preconceived notions regarding the subject would surely be shattered. Proof may remain elusive, but given these types of reports, the case for the Missouri Bigfoot remains open.

Alien Agenda

A more radical theory which swirls around the Momo case is that of extraterrestrial origin. Advocates of this idea suggest it would not only explain the unique anatomy of the beast (i.e., the alleged pumpkin-shaped head), but account for the UFO activity going on at the same time it was sighted. This alien theory was popular from the outset and in many ways drove the initial investigation since much of the research was done by UFO enthusiasts who believed there was some connection between the two phenomena. Perhaps the "craft" were dropping off an "experimental animal," as Hayden Hewes once put it, which closely resembled our concept of Bigfoot.

While the co-mingling of the aerial phenomenon and the creature sightings is interesting, it leaps even further into a quagmire of supposition since no one reportedly saw the creature exiting or entering any type of craft. Not to mention, there's no proof that the glowing lights and/or alleged crafts themselves were of extraterrestrial origin. The only thing we can say for sure is there are some documented reports where hairy bipeds have been seen during flaps of strange, skyward activity. This sort of "high strangeness" (as it has come to be known) can be found in cases such as Pennsylvania's Chestnut Ridge, as we've already explored, along with others including the Bridgewater Triangle in Massachusetts and the famed Skinwalker Ranch in Utah, where just about every type of paranormal phenomena has been represented from balls of light to hairy cryptids.

This combination may seem new in terms of "flying saucers," however, such things can be traced all the way back to Native American tales. According to longtime paranormal researcher and author, Brad Steiger, he obtained a copy of a journal written by the grandfather of James C. Wyatt in 1888.[106] In the journal, Wyatt's grandfather states that he and several cowhands had been forced to spend a winter with an Indian tribe who lived along the "Humboldt Line" in what he called the "Big Woods Country." (Presumably, this would be the Humboldt Meridian Line or Humboldt County Line located in northern California.) His grandfather was fluent in many tribal languages and proficient in sign language, so he was presumably able to communicate effectively with members of the tribe.

One day during their stay, Wyatt's grandfather said he noticed a tribesman carrying a "large platter of raw meat." When asked about the purpose, the Indian invited the cattleman to follow him to a cave in a nearby cliff face. When they arrived, the cattleman was stunned to see some sort of beast with "long, shiny black hair that covered its entire body, except for the palms and an area around its eyes." It was very man-like, yet was more muscular and didn't appear to have much of a neck. "The creature's head seemed to rest directly on its shoulders," as he put it.

Despite its wild appearance, it seemed fairly docile. When the Indian presented the platter of meat, it simply sat down and ate it.

Wyatt's grandfather was intently curious about the origin

of the bizarre creature and after much pleading and questioning, one of the men from the tribe finally told him the story. He said the thing was called "Crazy Bear" and had been brought to the "Big Woods" from the stars by a "small moon." The small moon "had flown down like a swooping eagle and had landed on a plateau a few miles away from the tribe's encampment." The Crazy Bear and two others like it were "flung" from the "small moon" before it flew off again back to the stars.

The creatures were subsequently led to the village by some tribesman, "and at no time had the hairy giants offered any resistance to their benefactors." The tribe believed the creatures had been sent to bring them "powerful medicine" and therefore they took great care to protect and feed them.

Were these creatures real and did they come from "the stars"? Given the nature of Native American folklore and spirit animals, we may never know.

In modern times, there are other examples in which glowing lights similar to what was reported in the Momo case coexist with reports of Bigfoot-like creatures. One of these originates from an area near my home in Texas. The place is located in the Big Thicket of East Texas along a dusty thoroughfare known as Bragg Road, or as it is often called, "Ghost Road." Witnesses here have not only claimed to see a glowing light which appears to hover and fly among the trees, but also a hairy biped.

The light phenomenon – which was originally dubbed "The Saratoga Light" due to the location's proximity to Saratoga, Texas – has become so well-known that people come from all around Texas and the surrounding states hoping to see it for themselves. Skeptics have routinely dismissed the phenomenon as either car headlights or swamp gas, or jokingly referred to them as the "Bud Lights" since they equate the sightings with the consumption of beer. Eyewitnesses, however, say otherwise.

In a dramatic incident documented by my late friend and fellow Texan, Rob Riggs, Roxanne Keubodeaux said she and her family were driving along Bragg Road one night when a strange light suddenly appeared in their path.[107] She abruptly swerved and stopped the truck, thinking it was an oncoming car driving recklessly down the road. As they sat there, confused and bewildered, the light began to hover over their vehicle's hood. Suddenly, the engine went dead. When the light finally zoomed off they found a strange burn mark in the hood's paint.

In another case, a longtime hunter in the area by the name of Mr. Boudreaux told Riggs he had grown up in the area and flat-out didn't believe in the ghostlight stories.... until the night he saw it himself. Boudreaux said he and some other guys were on a night-time hunt for razorback hogs in the area of Hardin County when they noticed a light in the distance.[108] At first they dismissed it as car headlights, but within a short time the light was much closer and much larger in size.

The men began to grow nervous, thinking it was a game warden on his way to bust them for what was essentially an illegal hunt since it was after dark. However, once the light was right on top of the hunters, they realized it was the infamous phantom orb. The light moved ominously in the air above them as they scrambled into their truck and tore out of the woods. It was the last time Boudreaux would laugh off such tales.

I received a more recent report from Gregory Pletcher, who said he was scared out of the very same woods in November 2004. On the evening in question, Pletcher said he and his brother had gone deer hunting at their lease near Bragg Road. They only had one ATV, so his brother dropped him off at his stand first before driving to his own. Pletcher proceeded to hunt until dark when he finally gave up and climbed down from his stand. At that point, he tried to call his brother to let him know he was ready to be picked up, but the connection failed. Shortly thereafter, he heard the ATV driving off in the distance, apparently leaving him on his own.

Pletcher said he started walking back to camp, which was

a considerable distance away. Eventually the trail he was using met up with Bragg Road. As he walked down the old road he could hear the nocturnal sound of animals moving in the brush, but it was so dark he couldn't see much beyond the end of his gun barrel. The night took on an eerie ambiance.

"I had been walking for maybe 20-25 minutes when a small light appeared about 15-20 yards off to the left side of the road," Pletcher said. "The light was low to the ground, as if someone were laying down holding a penlight pointing in my direction." The hunter's first thought was that someone was hiding there. He shouted and held up his rifle, but there was no response. That's when things took a fast and frightening turn.

Suddenly, the light was right in front of him, much larger than it was before. "I realized my gun was going to do me no good at this point so I turned and ran as fast as I could the way I'd just come from," Pletcher explained. "I can recall a reddish-orange glow that was chasing me down this road. I must have covered a mile in less than a minute's time."

As he ran, Pletcher noticed headlights moving up the trail through the woods. It was his brother on the ATV. As soon as the ATV was in sight, the strange light simply disappeared into the woods.

"When my brother got to me, I was hysterical just blabbering gibberish and terrified to tears," Pletcher admitted. "He thought I was attacked by something." When they reached camp, Pletcher told several other hunters what he'd seen. As you might guess, no one believed him.

As notable as the Saratoga Lights have become, it's not the only strange thing that's been seen in that stretch of Texas woods. The notorious Big Thicket also boasts a long history of encounters with a creature the locals often refer to as Ol' Mossyback. The description of this alleged beast is not unlike that of Momo or Bigfoot in general, with a purported hairy, ape-like body, ability to walk on two legs, and elusive nature.

In his book, *In the Big Thicket: On the Trail of the Wild Man*, Riggs recounts a story told to him by a witness named John. The young man said he was at his rural home one night when he heard a disturbance outside in his rabbit pens.[109] When he went out to investigate, he saw a "large, dark form" running towards the woods with one of his rabbits in hand. In the moonlight, John impulsively chased the mysterious thief, following the squeals of its hapless prey. Upon reaching the riverbank a short distance away, John said he watched "as what looked like a huge ape-like animal swam to the other side of the river, easily negotiating the strong current, and never letting go of the rabbit."

Several other men claim to have seen the ape-like creature in the Big Thicket Preserve close to Saratoga. On one occasion they saw it creeping around an old bridge at dusk. They were close enough to see it clearly walking in a bipedal fashion.

I personally interviewed a witness who saw a creature in

Primitive terrain of the Big Thicket
(Photo by Jerry Hestand)

the same area during the fall of 1972 (at the tail-end of the Momo frenzy no less!) According to Donna Gilchriest Grundy, who was twelve years old at the time, she was riding in the car with her grandmother and great aunt one afternoon around 3:30 p.m. as they traveled along a fire lane road in a heavily wooded area of the Big Thicket. The road was unpaved, so they were driving at a slow speed. As Donna was leaning forward from the back seat talking with her grandmother and great aunt, all three saw a large, hairy creature emerge from the woods and run across the road on two legs. It was so close, it missed the bumper by a mere three feet!

"It never looked at us, but we could see the body very well," Grundy told me in an interview. "It was covered in thick, long, shaggy hair that kind of shook on its body as it ran. It had long arms and a chest that was really thick."

The trio watched as the thing leaped over a drainage ditch at the side of the road and disappeared into the dense thicket. The creature ran in a slightly hunched-over fashion, swinging its arms as it went, and stayed on two legs the entire time. Grundy estimated its height to be seven to eight feet tall.

"We were stunned and shocked and pretty much afraid because we didn't know what we had just seen," she admitted. To her best recollection she had never heard anyone talk about Bigfoot in that part of Texas at the time. There was simply nothing else to compare it to aside from a "hairy monster."

While I've interviewed enough credible witnesses in the Big Thicket area (and even received an audio recording of a chilling, unexplained howl) to conclude that something strange is going on there, it's not enough to establish a solid connection between the light phenomenon and potential presence of an ape-like creature. As with Momo, no one has reportedly seen the alleged creature(s) exit from any sort of mechanical craft or glowing ball of light. And it's this very issue that seems to lie at the crux of this complicated quagmire. If the entity is actually an unknown sort of hairy biped, did it come from outer space or did the heightened awareness of one phenomenon cause people to pay more attention to something that would have otherwise been insignificant or unrelated?

The idea that mysterious, hairy bipeds (collectively known as Bigfoot) are actually aliens is something that's been hotly debated among cryptozoologists and ufologists for years. When stories of Sasquatch first grabbed the attention of researchers in the 1960s, the creatures were almost unanimously believed to be of biological, terrestrial origin. In other words, the creatures were thought to be either undocumented apes or relic hominids which had somehow existed under the radar of science. Later, as Bigfoot reports became more prominent in the 1970s and were often

Cover of the February 1973 issue of Flying Saucer Review

lumped in with reports of other "high strangeness" – such as ghost lights and UFOs – researchers such as Stan Gordon and John Keel proposed there may be a connection between these phenomena. As more UFO researchers began to look into Bigfoot reports, the boundary between the two subjects became even more blurred. This is evidenced in the Momo case where UFO researchers were investigating reports of what initially seemed like a Bigfoot.

The situation was exacerbated in the public's eye not only by the sensational news headlines, but by the co-mingling of such topics within books and articles co-authored by prominent cryptozoologist, Loren Coleman, and one of the foremost investigators of strange phenomenon, Jerome Clark. One such article, titled "Anthropoids, Monsters and UFOs" covered the very topic of Momo. When it appeared in the February 1973 issue of *Flying Saucer Review*, it resulted in an even more solid association between Momo and the subject of extraterrestrials.

Both Coleman and Clark have since rejected the pairing, as Coleman wrote in his authoritative book *Bigfoot! The True Story of Apes in America*, explaining that, regrettably: "This was an era in which several threads of the inexplicable overlapped, danced about together, and merged. It was an unfortunate marriage that still scars the field [of Bigfoot research]."[110]

Clark weighed in on the issue in his 1996 book, *High Strangeness: UFOs from 1960 through 1979*, when he noted that: "These are huge suppositions tied to small evidence" and "there is hardly anything about Hairy Bipeds, or their possible connections with the UFO phenomena, that can be stated with any degree of confidence."[111]

Hayden Hewes, whose contribution undoubtedly helped shape the early newsprint perception of Momo, is now deceased. As such, I was not able to solicit his view on the case as it stands today. However, by August 1972, he seemed to be in favor of a more terrestrial explanation for Momo as well. In a news conference held at his home on August 1, Hewes stated he believed the creature might be "an unknown form of hominid, much like the Neanderthal-like man thought to be extinct since pre-historic time."[112] He said that during his stay in Missouri he interviewed at least 20 persons who either saw, heard or smelled the alleged creature. "We are convinced something is there," he concluded.

To make matters more confusing, in recent years, the theory that Bigfoot creatures can be explained in terms of the paranormal has become increasing popular. Proponents of this theory believe they could be inter-dimensional beings which are seen only when moving through layers of a multi-dimensional universe. The idea was first expressed by John Keel, who is best known for his book *The Mothman Prophecies*. Keel suggested there may be "window areas" where bizarre creatures "materialize when lightning courses across the sky or certain magnetic conditions prevail. They are not real or physical in the usual sense," he said, "but they are real enough while they last."[113] This would account for the creatures' apparent abilities to avoid photography and fatal bullets. The outlook has often been applied to cases such as Momo where people have seemingly seen something, yet proof remains elusive.

It's understandable that more extreme explanations for Bigfoot creatures have gained a foothold over the years, considering we are virtually no closer to an absolute resolution than we were over 50 years ago when Roger Patterson and Bob Gimlin filmed the infamous Bigfoot footage at Bluff Creek. However, we must not underestimate the abilities of forest creatures to camouflage themselves for the purpose of remaining hidden. Much of North America's forests and swamps have been trod upon by humans, yet there are still pockets of deep woods where a creature, if it were to possess the right natural abilities and above average intelligence, could thrive. In other words, Momo could just as well have been an undiscovered beast as it was an otherworldly visitor. Or perhaps something else altogether. It seems the case is still open with one last, earthly and more mundane possibility.

Aping Around

If we rule out apes, aliens, and alter-reality entities, we're left with one more possible explanation to consider: that of a hoax. As tends to happen with these type of creature outbreaks, rumors eventually surface claiming the whole thing was hoaxed by one or more individuals. Momo is no exception.

From the get-go some of the locals dismissed the sightings as a simple case of teenage pranking. However, at the time nobody claimed responsibility. It was only years later that some of the rumors gained traction.

One of the first things that came under scrutiny was the footprint cast made at the Suddarth home on August 3, 1972. According to the original story, the footprints were discovered after Bill Suddarth went outside to investigate a strange howl. As he looked around, he was said to have noticed several large footprints in the family's garden. Believing they could have been made by Momo, he called his friend Clyde Penrod who brought plaster to make a cast.

The presence of a strange footprint and the resulting track cast are indeed real, however, the circumstance of the find and the origin of the print are quite different. While researching for this book, I spoke to Gail Suddarth, daughter of Bill Suddarth, who admitted a few years ago that she was in fact the maker of the infamous track.

Gail still resides in the town of Louisiana, not far from their former home on Dougherty-Pike Road, so I was able to meet with her in person during my visit there. She explained how the track came to be.

"I was eight-years-old at the time and everyone had been talking about Momo; it's all they talked about," Gail began. "We lived out in the country there, so of course I'd heard all the stories. My mom was even sure she'd actually seen it."

On the morning in question, Gail said she'd gone out early

to pick tomatoes in their garden. As she was plucking them from the vines, she looked down at the soft mud and got an idea. 'Why not make a monster track just for fun?'

"They'd estimated this creature to be so tall and weigh so much," she said, "so I just took my heel and stuck it down in the ground, you know, in a place for the heel, and a little bit less of an indentation for the middle, and then places for the toes. I did it all with my heel."

Once she was satisfied with her monster track, young Gail ran into the house and excitedly told her parents what she had "found." When they came outside and saw the bizarre footprint, they assumed it must have been connected to the alleged creature sightings. Before Gail knew it, her dad called Clyde Penrod and things quickly got out of hand.

"It became a big deal all of a sudden," Gail explained, "so I thought I'd be in trouble if I said anything. I just kept it to myself for years."

She kept it to herself for nearly 30 years, in fact, until she finally told her parents. Her mother was a bit skeptical since she believes she actually saw Momo on their property back then, but her father admitted he had suspicions all along. Either way, the cast was made and the incident became part of Momo's public record.

The cast, which is in the possession of Christina Windmiller (daughter of Clyde Penrod), doesn't look much like the footprint of an animal with its three, bulbous toes and odd shape. This was undoubtedly why Lawrence Curtis of the Oklahoma City Zoo rejected the prints as "fakes," although in his opinion they had been made by "someone wearing either rubber gloves or mittens" instead of using their foot, as Gail actually did.[114] Either way, ruling the footprint out is actually a positive step towards evaluating the entirety of the case. It never really seemed like a plausible creature track, and in the end, it wasn't. It was simply a child's crude contribution to something that has yet to be fully explained.

Stories about a much larger-scale hoax have also circulated among the townsfolk, although actual names have never been attached to the claims. According to Priscilla Giltner, a retired school teacher in the area, the totality of Momo can be attributed to the work of three boys who were in high school at the time. According to Giltner, "the boys fashioned a homemade monster suit they used only sporadically. They made the curious noises, planted the fake footprints and concocted the putrid smells."[115]

Giltner, whose explanation was included in a 2012 article published by the *Columbia Daily Tribune*, wouldn't reveal any names, but did conjecture on their motivation to keep quiet all this time. "I don't think they planned for it to get as big as it did," she said. "They were just bored."

Revelations like these may seem like a fatal blow to the case, but Momo would not be the first cryptid stricken with claims of unproven hoaxery. The claims rarely come with proof – such as the alleged costume – or explanations as to how someone could have pulled off such a feat while hundreds of townsfolk, police, and outside investigators were scouring the countryside with flashlights and shotguns. Not to mention, who was responsible for the other ape-like creature sightings which took place in a fairly wide radius over a period of several years?

I've seen similarities in cases such as the Lake Worth Monster and the Bishopville Lizard Man where various locals – and even people who lived in the surrounding cities at the time – will tell you they know "the real story." They generally cite the most popular rumor, which in the case of the Lizard Man was that a farmer had been responsible for the "incident." However, these folks don't seem to be aware there were multiple incidents. If they are aware of the other reports, they seem to be satisfied that a farmer would have no problem jumping on cars, running across the highway in the early-morning hours, and slogging through swamps for several years in order to perpetuate the entirety of the affair. Not to mention, more than one individual has claimed to be responsible for the most infamous incident where the "Lizard Man" allegedly attacked a teenager. Even the claims of hoaxes contradict the facts in the case and never account for the whole of the phenomenon. It's a pattern I've seen repeated over and over in these small town monster cases where the boasts of responsibility are nearly as unbelievable as the possibility of a mysterious monster itself.

In the case of Momo, it's not impossible that some kids fashioned a crude costume and pulled off some pranks. However, if so, they did some impressive work. The two women who were picnicking saw the "ape-like creature" in broad daylight and within a very close proximity as it stood outside their car window while they were locked inside. Granted they were frightened, but at this close of a range how could they mistake a homemade costume for a real animal? It seems unlikely that any costume short of a professional level construct would have been good enough to fool two adult witnesses in broad daylight. It might have worked in the case of the Harrison kids, who were younger and viewing "the creature" from a greater distance, but in the case of the picnickers? How could it? Not to mention the bravery that would have been required of the hoaxer(s). Walking up on old timers such as Ellis Minor on River Road in the dark or running across farmer's fields in the early morning hours seems like a risky proposition considering they could have easily been shot.

The lingering odor is another head scratcher. All the witnesses who smelled the odor agreed it was extraordinarily putrid and powerful. If it was concocted by pranksters, then it would have required them to use something on the level of a skunk's spray or perhaps a dead animal. Sounds like a lot of mess and trouble for a simple prank. Again, it's not impossible, just something to consider.

I think the biggest question here in regard to the hoax scenario is how to account for the totality of the incidents which are not simply confined to the boundaries of the small town. Kids might do funny stuff when they're bored, but were they running up and down the Mississippi basin for years donning a costume? What was it the fishermen saw wading in the Cuivre River? What did other witnesses see in and around Missouri and Illinois in the years before and after the headline-grabbing Momo scare? It's a question that remains to be answered.

While it's possible some kids pulled off a hoax in the case of Momo, ultimately without identities or other tangible items to back up third-party claims and rumors, it only adds another piece to a puzzling case which, to this day, still remains officially unsolved.

CONCLUSION

As I drove through the quiet streets below Marzolf Hill I wondered how many of the residents there still thought about the story, or even knew of it. I had come a long way from Texas to visit what is essentially their backyard for the purpose of a "monster" story. But it was important as an investigator and journalist to see the area for myself. Even though it happened a long time ago, just visiting the town and its significant locations would provide a perspective I would not have had otherwise. I'd read about Momo in books, I'd seen all the newspapers and blog posts, but being there added a whole new dimension.

After a few blocks I came to the intersection of Allen Street and turned left. The road looked as ordinary as any of them, but it was one of the most significant. At the end of Allen Street is where the Harrison family lived during that time. I already knew the house was gone (Doris told me during our conversation) but I would still be able to see the spot where their encounter had occurred.

I passed three or four houses as I proceeded to the end of the road, which literally dead-ends into Marzolf Hill. I drove up and parked at the edge of the woods and got out. Directly in front of me was a trail leading up the hill; to my right a section of mowed grass and a small picnic table which overlooked Dougherty-Pike Road and Highway 54 below it.

To my left, I could see the place where the Harrison's house had once stood. Doris told me their old barbecue grill was still there, and sure enough, I could see part of its black underbelly poking out of the underbrush next to a large tree. The grill had

The front of the former Harrison property
(Notice the barbecue grill just to the left of the large tree)
(Photo by Lyle Blackburn)

nearly succumbed to the foliage, yet managed to remain visible as if it were some forgotten historical marker.

I walked past the grill to the vacant lot, which is now just an overgrown spot next to the woods. The scant remains of a few rotting frame-boards were all that appeared to be left of the old house. Like the family's barbecue cooker, they too were being overtaken by time and nature.

I looked to the trees at the base of the hill. It was there the black-haired thing had stood on that fateful summer day back in 1972. I thought about the unlikely circumstances. Regardless of whether it was an otherworldly creature, a Bigfoot, or just a kid in a costume, the story that launched from that little spot has been catapulted worldwide. It was something that couldn't have been predicted or planned. It was something that simply happened in that brief moment, leaving us to wonder about its true nature nearly 50 years later.

I walked across the old lot, past a trashed-out boat, to the edge of the silent trees. A wall of leaves and brush still obscured any view of the hill which lay just beyond. The woods had obviously encroached even more over the years, illustrating the wild nature of the location. I turned around and looked back at the spot where the former house had once stood. I imagined how frightened the boys must have been, and the panic poor Doris had surely felt when she looked out the bathroom window to see a massive, hair-covered thing standing only feet from where her screaming brothers had been playing. It was not something one expects to see on a lazy summer day, even when living on the edge of nature's wildest boundaries.

After a few minutes of contemplation, I walked back to the pile of old boards and began rummaging around. I was in the habit of bringing back souvenirs from my journeys and one of these would be absolutely perfect. (Nothing spices up living room décor like rotting boards and bricks from the locations of famous cryptid cases!) Most of the boards were rather large, but I finally located one small enough to fit in the car. When I reached down to grab it, I found that it was held fast within the grasp of the foliage. As I was trying to free it, I glanced over at the nearest home. From where I stood I could see the side and back of the house. It wasn't too close, but it wasn't far and it wasn't fenced off either. I realized that from my position it might appear as though I was a trespasser. I'd poked around in the woods near plenty of rural homes, so I was familiar with the protective habits (if you will) of the residents. I hurried to collect the board, hoping I wouldn't end up having to run at the sound of a shotgun blast.

Once I had the board – which was quite decayed from moisture and insects – I headed over to toss it in the car. For a moment I thought about the barbecue grill, but decided not to try. Not only was it serving as a historical marker, but I would probably have a hell of a time trying to get it out of there. Shotgun blasts would surely ring out if I started ransacking the lot as if I were collecting items for an antique show!

After stashing my wooden souvenir in the car, I turned my attention to the path leading up onto Marzolf Hill. It was well-defined and appeared to have been there a long time. I pictured the frenzy of the search parties as they headed up there clutching their weapons. I'm sure most of the men had their doubts about a monster, but still, no one really knew what to expect. It was like a scene from an old horror-sci-fi movie where the gut reaction is to

Path leading onto Marzolf Hill
(Photo by Lyle Blackburn)

seek out the beast and kill it. It seems laughable in terms of those old movies, but of course this wasn't a movie; it was real life.

I proceeded up the path which tunneled through the trees. The incline was gradual, and at first it seemed like the hike was going to be relatively easy. However, the path only went up about 40 yards before it was abruptly cut off and surrounded by dense brush and trees. I stopped and peered into the shadowy canopy. I was just beyond a city street, yet I was already enveloped by what appeared to be very substantial woods.

Formidable woodlands are nothing new, of course, so I bid the worthless trail goodbye and trudged into the midst of un-bridled nature. I wasn't in search of anything particular, just trying to get a sense of whether the vicinity would be suitable for large animals, or at least afford sufficient places to hide.

As I continued up and around the hill, it didn't take long to make my conclusion. The trees were decidedly thick and un-ruly, and I found myself periodically fighting through tangles of underlying flora to keep on track. I didn't see much in the way of wildlife, but if something did take up residence here it wouldn't be hard to conceal itself within the folds. The only problem, I felt, would have been getting to and from the location. It was like a primitive island in the midst of houses, farms, roads, and train tracks.

I leveled off at what seemed to be the maximum height of the hill so I started working back around in a crescent-moon arch. Along the way I came upon some heaps of trash which appeared to be old dumping sites. It was no doubt similar to the refuge inves-tigators encountered at the time. I didn't find any old buildings, but it's not to say they weren't there. Something could've easily been overtaken and pulled back into the clutches of nature, just as the Harrison's old lot had. Many years had gone by, so inevitably much had changed. Marzolf Hill had become increasingly cut off from its countryside surroundings, yet within its own heart, it still seemed wild.

I eventually made it back to the short trail and descended down the hill. By the time I got to my car, I was covered in sweat and probably every chigger Marzolf had to offer. But it didn't matter. I had done my due diligence as a journalist, while at the same time satisfying that old flame of childhood curiosity. I'd walked on the legendary hill I'd read so much about. As a focal point, it was as crucial to the story as the alleged beast itself.

The sun was now making its descent toward the western horizon as the afternoon burned away. I still had one more thing to do, so I brushed off and got back in the car. From Allen Street I drove a short distance to Highway 79 and proceeded north, away from town and opposite from the direction I'd come in. As if in reverse, the townscape quickly faded back to countryside where trees and farmland took over again. The houses on this stretch looked more affluent as they sat nestled in large tracts of rolling hills and green grass. Atop one of the road's high crests, I could see for miles across the outskirts of town.

I went on a bit further until I came to a road which branched north from the curving Highway 79 into what appeared to be another heavily wooded area. I turned and drove into its swath of dense trees. Along the way I saw examples of the karst, limestone bluffs which marked the area along the river basin. It was more wild country sandwiched between the farms, water, and rolling highways.

After the detour, I wound back to Highway 79 and resumed my drive away from town. Now I began to scan the road for a scenic turnout. I knew it was somewhere along this stretch that the picnickers had their dramatic encounter with the resident monster. I drove slowly, keeping my eye out, but didn't see any such location. Was it gone?

I did a U-turn and retraced the route, looking even more carefully this time. My slow procession was starting to annoy a few drivers which had come up behind me. One of them honked. I didn't blame them though. How could they have possibly known about my important mission?!

Finally, I caught sight of what looked like an old piece of road jutting off at an angle from the highway. I looped around again and turned onto it. The pavement was faded and crumbling from the exposed heat of the years. I stopped the car and consulted my map. There were no trees or picnic tables, but this had to be it.

I got out of the car and looked around. A huge crop field stretched to the north, while a row of scattered trees stood to the east. If this was it, it was nothing like it had been back in 1972. There wasn't even an unofficial historical marker like I'd found at the Harrison's old lot. No scrap of table wood or clump of bushes left to signify the site where the Momo mystery had quietly started all those years ago.

As I looked out across the pastoral peacefulness, I laughed to myself. The cars that meandered by probably thought I was lost; some confused individual taking a respite from a long Midwest journey. Just like those poor women who took a break to enjoy a nice lunch, but instead got the scare of their lives.

And perhaps I was a little bit crazy for wanting to visit this old place and write a book about its would-be monster. It wasn't the most celebrated story of the 1970s; it wasn't the most relevant; heck, it might've even been a hoax. However, that's not the point. Something had taken place at this very site which added fuel to a mystery that's ignited imaginations worldwide. A mystery that brought waves of journalists, researchers, and hunters to a small town during a time when perhaps folks needed a bit of light-hearted fun. Concerns over politics and the counter-culture movement were high in those days, and the horrors of the Vietnam War were all too real. Perhaps Midwest America was in need of something that evoked a bit of spooky charm and mystery, even if it came from a hill in their own backyard.

The 1970s would go on to become something of a "golden

age" in terms of these strange tales – from cryptid beasts to UFOs to ghosts. And at the forefront was one of the most memorable: Momo, the Missouri Monster.

I looked down at the cracked pavement and over to the row of trees whose afternoon shadows were beginning to stretch like old memories. I knew I was far too late for a chance encounter with the hairy legend, but I was not too late to finally write its complete story.

Last remains of the paved scenic turnout
(Photo by Lyle Blackburn)

ACKNOWLEDGEMENTS

Special thanks to Loren Coleman, Jerome Clark, and the late Richard Crowe for their timely documentation of these events. Without their work, crucial details of the case would have been lost.

Thanks to the following colleagues, friends, and other individuals who have supported my efforts and contributed to this book:

Sandy Blackburn, Ray Castile, Marc DeWerth, Aaron Fraser, Ken Gerhard, Stan Gordon, Bobby Hamilton (GCBRO), Veronica Hernandez, Jerry Hestand, Cindy Lee, Kevin Linke, Matt Moneymaker (BFRO), Daniel Perez, Nick Redfern, Michael Rocco, Gail Suddarth, Dale Triplett, Anne Walls, David Weatherly, Christina Windmiller, and Craig Woolheater.

And thanks to all the witnesses and organizations who graciously shared their experiences and information.

APPENDIX

Maps

The following maps are included for reference.

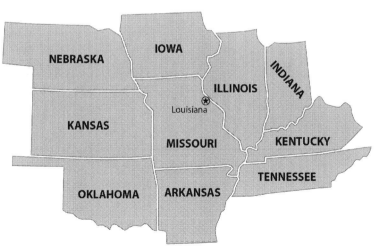

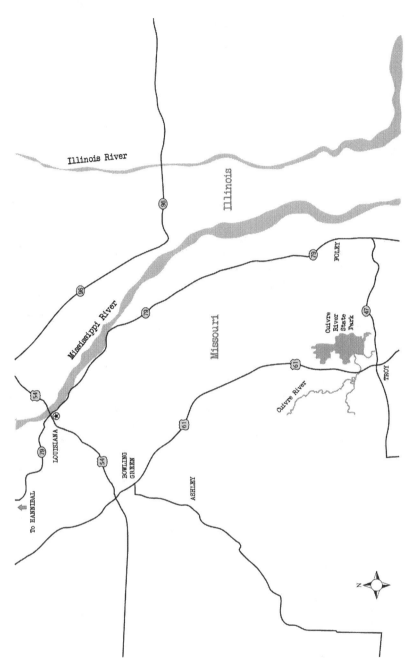

General area south of Louisiana, Missouri

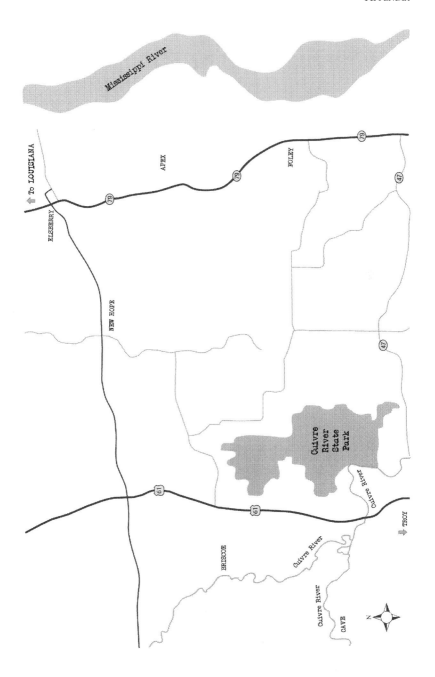

Cuivre River Area

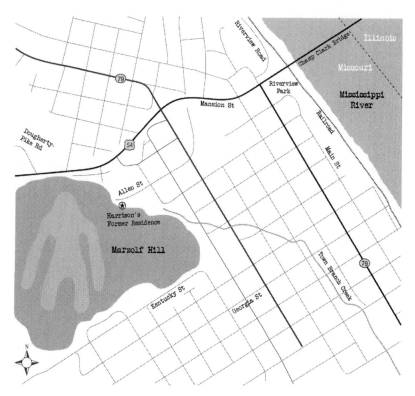

Louisiana, Missouri

Momo Incident Log

Summer 1970:   Louisiana, MO - Sighting of an "unknown creature" was allegedly reported to the Pike County Sheriff's Office.

July 1971:   Louisiana, MO - Joan Mills and Mary Ryan were having a picnic at a scenic turnout just north of town when a hairy, ape-like creature emerged from the woods and approached them. The frightened women fled to their car until the creature eventually returned to the woods.

July 1971:   Louisiana, MO - A young man supposedly saw a "big, tall, black ugly thing" in the vicinity of an abandoned school.

June 30, 1972:   Troy, MO at Cuivre River (approximately 20 miles south of Louisiana) - Two fisherman saw a tall, hairy creature wade across the river and walk up on the bank approximately 150 feet away. At first they thought it was a person with long hair, but when it came out of the water and started to approach they realized it was some kind of animal. The same evening, another couple fishing upstream heard some kind of strange "grunts and groans."

July 1972:   (Prior to July 11) Louisiana, MO - A farmer named Wendorff watched a dark, humanoid figure walk across his field in the direction of the Mississippi River. It walked with "an odd, shuffling gait" and looked something like "a very large old man wearing a fur overcoat." Later that afternoon, Wendorff found a set of "strange tracks" leading down to the riverbank.

July 11, 1972:   Louisiana, MO - Doris (15), Terry (8), and Walley (5) Harrison saw a tall, upright hair-covered creature in their backyard at the foot of Marzolf Hill. The thing had no neck and a large, pumpkin-sized head, and reeked with a terrible odor. It held what appeared to be a dead dog in its arms.

July 11, 1972:   Louisiana, MO - Mrs. Clarence Lee heard a "terrible, growling animal sound" in the vicinity of the Harrison home. Robert E. Parsons and his wife also heard the strange sound from a distance.

July 14, 1972:   Louisiana, MO - A dozen people, including Edgar Harrison saw several "balls of light" move from east to west, just over the trees in the neighboring yard. They saw two others – one white and one green – go down in the vicinity of a nearby school. A short time later, Harrison and his family heard something that sounded like a loud growl. As it got closer and closer, the family fled in their car. Edgar Harrison and Maxine Minor reported the incidents to police.

July 15, 1972:   Pike County, MO - Bill Riley was allegedly chased by a tall, humanoid creature covered in thick, matted hair. It gave off a horrible stench and let out a blood-curdling scream.

July 18, 1972:   Louisiana, MO - Two boys spotted an upright, hairy creature standing in the woods on Marzolf Hill. Around the same time, a woman told television reporters she had definitely seen a "black, long-haired thing" cross the highway into Louisiana. Yet another resident told police he also saw the thing near Highway 79, and it appeared to be carrying a sheep or dog in its mouth.

July 19, 1972:   Louisiana, MO - A group of 20 men - which included eight police officers, a State Conservation Officer, Edgar Harrison, four out-of-state reporters, and some local volunteers - combed the woods of Marzolf Hill in search of the creature or other evidence. Nothing was found.

July 19, 1972:   Louisiana, MO - Nearly 40 people heard an animal growling and roaring near Dougherty-Pike Road. The animal could not be identified.

July 20, 1972:   Louisiana, MO - Reporter Richard Crowe arrived on scene to investigate for *FATE* magazine. Edgar Harrison and Richard Bliss led Crowe onto Marzolf Hill where they came upon what appeared to be two large, human-like footprints. A short time later, they smelled an overwhelming stench which they suspected might have come from the "creature."

July 20, 1972:   New Haven, MO (approximately 58 miles south of Louisiana) – A female witness saw a gray-colored, hairy creature walking upright in a field during the early morning hours.

July 21, 1972:   Louisiana, MO - Ellis Minor was sitting in front of his house on River Road when he spotted a six-foot-tall, hair-covered thing walking towards the river. When he shined his flashlight on it, the thing ran back into the woods.

July 21, 1972:   Louisiana, MO - Teenager, Timmy McCormick, said he saw the "creature" in the woods surrounding the town.

July 24, 1972:   O'Fallon, MO (approximately 48 miles south of Louisiana) - Two teenage girls saw a "bear-like creature" walking upright near a wooded area outside of town.

July 26, 1972:   Louisiana, MO - Witnesses spotted a "fireball" land or hover atop a large tree near the railroad crossing on River Road (not far from where Ellis Minor claimed to have seen the creature). They said "two red spurts of light shot out from it" before it zoomed out of sight.

July 27, 1972:   Louisiana, MO - Witnesses (including members of the Harrison family and the Shade family) saw more colored lights above a bluff at the north end of River Road. These lights appeared to be "signaling back and forth" to each other. Mrs. Lois Shade (Edgar Harrison's sister) estimated they were "about the size of an apple."

July 29, 1972:   Louisiana, MO - Edgar Harrison and several local college students were exploring Marzolf Hill when they distinctly heard an "old man's voice" warning them to stay out of the woods. When they searched the small area of trees where the voice originated, no one could be found.

July 30, 1972: Louisiana, MO - Members of the Shade family saw another strange light or craft hovering over a thicket at the top of another bluff. Earnest Shade described it as being orange at first, then later changing to red and gray. His wife, Lois, said "it was disc-shaped" and had what appeared to be lighted "windows." The UFO remained there for several hours then suddenly gave off a "red glow" before it "went straight up into the air and disappeared."

July 31, 1972: Louisiana, MO - A set of mysterious footprints was found by Freddie Robbins on his farm eight miles south of town. They were roughly oval shaped and appeared to have three long, thin toes.

July/Aug 1972: Potosi, MO (approximately 150 miles south of Louisiana) - Two camp counselors chased a large, foul-smelling bipedal entity down a thickly wooded hillside at night. It moved so quickly and with such ease through the woods, they concluded it was not human. After hearing about the Momo sightings more than a year later, they couldn't help but note the similarities to what they saw.

Aug 3, 1972: Louisiana, MO - Bill Suddarth found a strange footprint in the garden outside their home on Dougherty-Pike Road. It was a large, bulbous looking track with three toes. The footprint was cast by Clyde Penrod. (The track was later determined to be a fabrication by Gail Suddarth, the young daughter of Bill Suddarth.)

Aug 4, 1972:   Louisiana, MO - Ernest Shade (16), Rossie Shade (7), Lewis Harrison (13), and Fred Harrison (10) were fishing at the Salt River (a tributary of the Mississippi River) when they saw a large, dark object moving upstream against the current. It appeared to be an animal with a head "bigger than a human" and shoulders which were "sticking out of the water" as it swam. They thought it might be a bear, but they weren't close enough to say for sure.

Aug 5, 1972:   Louisiana, MO - Pat Howard (who saw a dark, man-like figure on the morning of July 15) and a friend were camping in the Harrison's backyard sipping coffee when they heard a strange voice say: "I'll take a cup of your coffee." They conducted an immediate search of the area, but found no one. The disembodied voice was reminiscent of the one reported by Harrison and the college students a few weeks earlier.

Sept 8, 1972:   Louisiana, MO - James Davis saw a "large man" running near his house on Highway 79. Some theorized it might have been Momo, but Davis felt it was actually a person.

Oct 29, 1972:   Chestline, IL (approximately 27 miles northeast of Louisiana) - John Roman was surprised by a seven-foot-tall, hair-covered animal while camping. He described it as being brownish in color with very bulky, wide shoulders and a face which looked "more human than ape." After a few moments it ran away on two legs down a slope.

April 1973:   Louisiana, MO - A family was picking wild mushrooms in a deep hollow on the outskirts of Louisiana when they got wind of a horrible smell. A short time later, they heard an "unusual scream" coming from the same area. When discussing it with the grandmother, she said she had seen what looked like a "7-8 foot tall, hairy creature standing on its hind legs" outside her rural home. It left 15-inch long footprints in the soil.

Summer 1974:   Calhoun County, IL (approximately 30 miles from Louisiana) - Two men who were stopped on the Mississippi River Road smelled a horrible odor before catching sight of a "dark, tall, wide figure" watching them in the dark. They did not think it was a person.

1974:   Pike County, MO – A man was driving near Battle Creek in the early morning hours when he saw a large, human-like figure come from the woods and run across the road. It appeared to be covered in dark hair, and was tall and ape-like, yet stayed upright on two feet the entire time.

1991:   Pike County, MO - A man camping in the woods on his family's property saw a large, ape-like creature squatting in a creek. After watching it for about 30 seconds, it jumped up and ran away.

Nov 16, 2007:   Pike County, IL (approximately 10 miles from Louisiana) - A hunter in a tree stand saw a large, hairy animal walking upright with huge strides. Its muscular body was covered in dark, rusty-brown hair and it had long arms, broad shoulders, and relatively no neck. The hunter was certain it was not a man.

Missouri Monster Links

"Momo the Missouri Monster" song by Bill Whyte:

https://billwhyte.bandcamp.com/track/mo-mo-the-missouri-monster

"The Shaggy Momo Beast" episode teaser from the *Monsters and Mysteries in America* television show:

https://youtu.be/pemtvMBxRJY

Momo Stalks the Midwest article by Raymond Castile:

www.stateofhorror.com/momo.html

Art Files

Momo-related blog posts and articles are often accompanied by images which have come to represent Momo in the modern age. The most prominent of these images is a drawing by illustrator Hal D. Crawford which depicts a rather wide, hairy biped with a huge head and glowing eyes. The image has become something of a recognizable icon in terms of cryptids, yet it was not a drawing of Momo per se. Crawford actually created the illustration prior to the Momo flap as part of a 1970 book titled *The Aliens* by Crawford, Hayden Hewes, and Kietha Hewes. In the book, the illustration depicts what the authors considered to be a type of alien. It was only later that the image came to represent Momo, presumably because it looks similar to the creature reported by some of the witnesses.

"Type 3" Alien
(Credit: Hal Crawford)

Drawings which accompanied Momo-related advertising in local newspapers were unique and entertaining. They were often used in combination with restaurant specials and department store sales.

Momo Interpretations
(Credit: Louisiana Press-Journal)

Photo Files

The following photos were taken during the author's trip to Louisiana, Missouri.

The author at the Louisiana sign on the Mississippi River (Blackburn)

Swing bridge over the Mississippi River (Blackburn)

Downtown Louisiana (Blackburn)

Railroad tracks on the edge of the Mississippi River (Blackburn)

Winding road just outside of town (Blackburn)

*The spot where "Momo" was seen by the Harrison kids in 1972
(Blackburn)*

ENDNOTES

1   Clark, Jerome and Loren Coleman. "Anthropoids, Monsters and UFOs." *Flying Saucer Review*, Vol. 19, No. 1, Jan-Feb 1973: 19-20. (The report was originally uncovered by Loren Coleman via law enforcement informants.)

2   Clark, Jerome and Loren Coleman. "Anthropoids, Monsters and UFOs." *Flying Saucer Review*, Vol. 19, No. 1, Jan-Feb 1973: 20-21.

3   Uhlenbrock, Thomas. "Monster Creates Excitement." *The Coshocton Tribune* 28 July 1972.

4   Steiger, Brad. *Mysteries of Time and Space*. New York: Dell Publishing Company, 1974. p. 107.

5   "Strange Sounds On Marzolf Hill Terrify Residents." *The Louisiana Press-Journal* 18 July 1972.

6   "Strange Sounds On Marzolf Hill Terrify Residents." *The Louisiana Press-Journal* 18 July 1972.

7   "Strange Sounds On Marzolf Hill Terrify Residents." *The Louisiana Press-Journal* 18 July 1972.

8   Clark, Jerome and Loren Coleman. "Anthropoids, Monsters and UFOs." *Flying Saucer Review*, Vol. 19, No. 1, Jan-Feb 1973: 21.

9   "Strange Sounds On Marzolf Hill Terrify Residents." *The Louisiana Press-Journal* 18 July 1972.

10   Clark, Jerome and Loren Coleman. "Anthropoids, Monsters and UFOs." *Flying Saucer Review*, Vol. 19, No. 1, Jan-Feb 1973: 21.

11   "'Mystery Beast' Terrorizes Town." *Nevada State Journal* 20 Jul 1972.

12   "The 'Monster' Becomes Famous – Search Party Finds Not A Trace." *The Louisiana Press-Journal* 20 July 1972.

13   Steiger, Brad. *Mysteries of Time and Space*. New York: Dell Publishing Company, 1974. p. 109.

14   Langleben, Tina. "Mysterious Hairy Monster Terrorizes a Town." *The National Enquirer* 1972.

15   "The 'Monster' Becomes Famous – Search Party Finds Not A Trace." *The Louisiana Press-Journal* 20 July 1972.

16   Crowe, Richard. "Monster in Missouri." *FATE*, Vol. 25, No. 12, Dec 1972: 61.

17   "Strange Sounds On Marzolf Hill Terrify Residents." *The Louisiana Press-Journal* 18 July 1972.

18   Crowe, Richard. "Monster in Missouri." *FATE*, Vol. 25, No. 12, Dec 1972: 61.

19   Crowe, Richard. "Monster in Missouri." *FATE*, Vol. 25, No. 12, Dec 1972: 61.

20   Crowe, Richard. "Monster in Missouri." *FATE*, Vol. 25, No. 12, Dec 1972: 61.

21   Crowe, Richard. "Monster in Missouri." *FATE*, Vol. 25, No. 12, Dec 1972: 62.

22   Uhlenbrock, Thomas. "Monster Creates Excitement." *The Coshocton Tribune* 28 July 1972.

23   Uhlenbrock, Thomas. "Monster Creates Excitement." *The Coshocton Tribune* 28 July 1972.

24   Langleben, Tina. "Mysterious Hairy Monster Terrorizes a Town." *The National Enquirer* 1972.

25   Crowe, Richard. "Monster in Missouri." *FATE*, Vol. 25, No. 12, Dec 1972: 64.

26   "'Mo-Mo Must Be Taken Alive' UFO Expert Says After Visit." *The Louisiana Press-Journal* 08 Aug 1972.

27   "'MoMo the Monster Sought by Authorities." *Pittsburg Post-Gazette* 31 Jul 1972.

28   "'Monster' Puts Louisiana On Map – St. Louis 70 Miles To South of Us." *The Louisiana Press-Journal* 01 Aug 1972.

29   "The 'Monster' Becomes Famous – Search Party Finds Not A Trace." *The Louisiana Press-Journal* 20 July 1972.

30   Baumann, Elwood D. *Monsters of North America*. Connecticut: Xerox Education Publications, 1978. p. 60

31   "The 'Monster' Becomes Famous – Search Party Finds Not A Trace." *The Louisiana Press-Journal* 20 July 1972.

32   "That Monster Is Still Around – So Are TV Men And UFO Experts." *The Louisiana Press-Journal* July 1972

33 "Monster Hunt – Jitters in Louisiana, Mo." *Associated Press*. July 1972

34 Steiger, Brad. *Mysteries of Time and Space*. New York: Dell Publishing Company, 1974. p. 107.

35 John Green Database (www.sasquatchdatabase.com).

36 Steiger, Brad. *Mysteries of Time and Space*. New York: Dell Publishing Company, 1974. p. 111.

37 Short, Norma E. "Mo Mo – That Missouri Monster." *Skylook MUFON UFO Journal*, Sept 09 1972: 5-8.

38 Steiger, Brad. *Mysteries of Time and Space*. New York: Dell Publishing Company, 1974. p. 112.

39 Bord, Janet and Colin. *Bigfoot Casebook Updated: Sightings and Encounters from 1818 to 2004*. Pine Winds Press, 2006 (first published in 1982). p. 266.

40 Baumann, Elwood D. *Monsters of North America*. Connecticut: Xerox Education Publications, 1978. pp. 49-51.

41 Warren, Brandy. "Momo mystery rears its head once more in Louisiana, Missouri." *St. Louis Post-Dispatch* 02 May 2001.

42 "Creature seen stepping over four foot barbed wire fence near the town of Louisiana." Bigfoot Field Research Organization Report #1136 (http://www.bfro.net/GDB/show_report.asp?id=1136)

43 "Man Reports Seeing 'Hairy Creature' In Woods Near Cole Hollow Road." *Pekin Daily Times* 26 Jul 1972.

44 "Woman Picking Berries Says She saw Monster Near Rt. 98 Thursday." *Pekin Daily Times* 28 Jul 1972.

45 Vogel, Nick. "Did a hairy monster stalk Tazewell County?" *Pekin Daily Times* 06 Nov 2006.

46 Bartels, DeWaye. "Cohomo is back." *East Peoria Times-Courier* 05 Jul 2012.

47 Clark, Jerome and Loren Coleman. "Anthropoids, Monsters and UFOs." *Flying Saucer Review*, Vol. 19, No. 1, Jan-Feb 1973: 21.

48 Crowe, Richard. "Monster in Missouri." *FATE*, Vol. 25, No. 12, Dec 1972: 65.

49 Crowe, Richard. "Monster in Missouri." *FATE*, Vol. 25, No. 12, Dec 1972: 65.

50   Crowe, Richard. "Monster in Missouri." *FATE*, Vol. 25, No. 12, Dec 1972: 66.

51   Crowe, Richard. "Monster in Missouri." *FATE*, Vol. 25, No. 12, Dec 1972: 63.

52   Rath, Jay. *The I-Files: True Reports of Unexplained Phenomena in Illinois*: Trails Books, Madison, 1999.

53   Clark, Jerome and Loren Coleman. "Anthropoids, Monsters and UFOs." *Flying Saucer Review*, Vol. 19, No. 1, Jan-Feb 1973: 21.

54   Moravec, Mark. *The UFO-Anthropoid Catalogue*: Arcturus Books Service, 1982.

55   Short, Norma E. "Large UFO 'Launches' Smaller Ones Over St. Louis County." *Skylook MUFON UFO Journal*, Sept 09 1972: 10.

56   Gordon, Stan. *Silent Invasion: The Pennsylvania UFO-Bigfoot Casebook*: self-published, Greensburg, 2010. p. 25.

57   Gordon, Stan. *Silent Invasion: The Pennsylvania UFO-Bigfoot Casebook*: self-published, Greensburg, 2010. p. 27.

58   Gordon, Stan. *Silent Invasion: The Pennsylvania UFO-Bigfoot Casebook*: self-published, Greensburg, 2010. p. 30

59   Gordon, Stan. *Silent Invasion: The Pennsylvania UFO-Bigfoot Casebook*: self-published, Greensburg, 2010. p. 96.

60   Gordon, Stan. *Silent Invasion: The Pennsylvania UFO-Bigfoot Casebook*: self-published, Greensburg, 2010. p. 133.

61   https://www.visitlouisianamo.com/about-louisiana-missouri/

62   http://greatriverroad.com/hannibal/louisiana.htm

63   http://greatriverroad.com/hannibal/louisiana.htm

64   *The History of Pike County, Missouri: An Encyclopedia of Useful Information, and a Compendium of Actual Facts*. Des Moines: Mills & Company, 1883. p. 711.

65   Koch, Augustus, Cartographer, Publisher Charles Shober & Co, and Lithographer Chicago Lithographing Co. Birds eye view of the city of Louisiana, Pike County, Mo. [Chicago: Chas. Shober & Co. Props., Chicago: Chicago Lith. Co, 1876] Map. Retrieved from the Library of Congress, <www.loc.gov/item/2015594060/>.

66 Allen, Betty Jane and Martha Sue Smith. *Images of America: Louisiana.* Charleston: Arcadia Publishing, 2012. p. 80.

67 Chapman, S.S., Omernik, J.M., Griffith, G.E., Schroeder, W.A., Nigh, T.A., and Wilton, T.F., 2002, Ecoregions of Iowa and Missouri (color poster with map, descriptive text, summary tables, and photographs): Reston, Virginia, U.S. Geological Survey (map scale 1:1,800,000).

68 Green, John. *Sasquatch: The Apes Among Us.* Washington/Vancouver: Hancock House, 1978. p. 196.

69 Green, John. *Sasquatch: The Apes Among Us.* Washington/Vancouver: Hancock House, 1978. p. 196.

70 Arment, Chad. *The Historical Bigfoot: Early Reports of Wild Men, Hairy Giants, and Wandering Gorillas in North America.* Landisville: Coachwhip Publications, 2006.

71 "Unknown Creature Sighted in Arkansas: Wild Man of the Woods" *The Memphis Enquirer* 09 May 1851.

72 "A Monstrous Wild Beast." *Iron County Register* 14 Apr 1881.

73 Twain, Mark. "The Wild Man Interviewed." *Buffalo Express* 18 Sep 1869.

74 "A Wild Man in Missouri." *Hornellsville Weekly Tribune* 19 Jun 1891.

75 "A Wild Man Roaming the Mills Near Sedalia, Mo., Causes Terror to Nervous People." *The Hamilton Daily Republican* 17 Sep 1894.

76 Green, John. *Sasquatch: The Apes Among Us.* Washington/Vancouver: Hancock House, 1978. p. 195.

77 "Recollections of numerous encounters at a logging camp during the Great Depression." Bigfoot Field Research Organization Report #24102 (http://www.bfro.net/GDB/show_report.asp?id=24102)

78 http://www.bigfootencounters.com/sbs/oldermissouri.htm

79 Keel, John A., *Strange Creatures From Time and Space.* Connecticut: Fawcett Publications, Inc., 1970. p. 111.

80 http://www.bigfootencounters.com/sbs/oldermissouri.htm

81 "Children see creature emerging from abandoned barn near Caruthersville." Bigfoot Field Research Organization Report #15610 (http://www.bfro.net/GDB/show_report.asp?id=15610)

82   "Childhood face to face encounter at dusk in the river bottoms of Bootheel." Bigfoot Field Research Organization Report #26962 (http://www.bfro.net/GDB/show_report.asp?id=26962)

83   Keel, John A., *Strange Creatures From Time and Space*. Connecticut: Fawcett Publications, Inc., 1970. p. 111.

84   http://www.gcbro.com/MOmonroe001.html

85   http://unsolvedmysteries.wikia.com/wiki/The_Ice_Man

86   "New Home Awaits Missouri Monster." *Great Bend Daily Tribune* 26 Jul 1972.

87   Montgomery, Dennis. "Farmers Hunt Chicken Man." *The Spokesman-Review* 01 Mar 1971.

88   "New Home Awaits Missouri Monster." *Great Bend Daily Tribune* 26 Jul 1972.

89   Crowe, Richard. "Monster in Missouri." *FATE*, Vol. 25, No. 12, Dec 1972: 62.

90   "Those Strange Sounds We Heard Last July Could Have Been By An Arkansas Bear." *The Louisiana Press-Journal* 05 Sept 1972.

91   "Those Strange Sounds We Heard Last July Could Have Been By An Arkansas Bear." *The Louisiana Press-Journal* 05 Sept 1972.

92   "'Monster' Puts Louisiana On Map – St. Louis 70 Miles To South of Us." *The Louisiana Press-Journal* 01 Aug 1972.

93   "'Monster' Puts Louisiana On Map – St. Louis 70 Miles To South of Us." *The Louisiana Press-Journal* 01 Aug 1972.

94   "Man recalls his face to face daylight encounter in Siloam Springs State Park." Bigfoot Field Research Organization Report #28423 (http://www.bfro.net/GDB/show_report.asp?id=28423)

95   "Family hears strange screams off Highway 54." Bigfoot Field Research Organization Report #5059 (http://www.bfro.net/GDB/show_report.asp?id=5059)

96   "Family hears strange screams off Highway 54." Bigfoot Field Research Organization Report #5059 (http://www.bfro.net/GDB/show_report.asp?id=5059)

97   "Memory told of a possible sighting on a back road west of Hardin." Bigfoot Field Research Organization Report #39827 (http://www.bfro.net/GDB/show_report.asp?id=39827)

98   Schremp Hahn, Valerie. "Jet Scream, MoMo the Monster, Mule-Go-Round and more: Six Flags attractions of yore." *St. Louis Post-Dispatch* 05 Jun 2018.

99   "Joplin's Hairy Monster Caught With Costume." *Lincoln Evening Journal* 01 Oct 1975.

100   Uhlenbrock, Thomas. "That Monster On Marzolf Hill." *Pekin Daily Times* 28 Jul 1972.

101   Richardson, Mark. "The Missouri Momo, a personal story by Mark Richardson now living in Modesto, California." (www.bigfootencounters.com/sbs/stcharles.htm)

102   "A man gathering firewood for his campsite with his ATV encounters a large ape-like animal in a creek bed." Bigfoot Field Research Organization Report #1135 (http://www.bfro.net/GDB/show_report.asp?id=1135).

103   Gillman, Joe. *Missouri – The Cave State*. Fact Sheet No. 15: Missouri Department of Natural Resources, Sept 2017.

104   Crews, Jeff "Dark Wonders: Karst, Caves and Springs in Missouri." *Missouri Resources*, Vol. 29, No. 1, Winter 2012, pp. 2-5.

105   "Hunter has sighting from his deer stand near Detroit." Bigfoot Field Research Organization Report #24354 (http://www.bfro.net/GDB/show_report.asp?id=24354)

106   Steiger, Brad. *Real Monsters, Gruesome Critters, and Beasts From the Darkside*. Canton: Visible Ink Press, 2011. pp. 247-248.

107   Riggs, Rob. *In the Big Thicket: On the Trail of the Wild Man*. New York: Paraview Press, 2001. p. 27.

108   Riggs, Rob. *In the Big Thicket: On the Trail of the Wild Man*. New York: Paraview Press, 2001. p. 27-28.

109   Riggs, Rob. *In the Big Thicket: On the Trail of the Wild Man*. New York: Paraview Press, 2001. p. 89.

110   Coleman, Loren. *Bigfoot! The True Story of Apes in America*. New York: Paraview Pocket Books, 2003. p. 170.

111   Clark, Jerome. *High Strangeness: UFOs from 1960 Through 1979*. Indiana: Omnigraphics, 1996. p. 221-222.

112 "'Mo-Mo Must Be Taken Alive' UFO Expert Says After Visit." *The Louisiana Press-Journal* 08 Aug 1972.

113 Keel, John A., *Strange Creatures From Time and Space*. Connecticut: Fawcett Publications, Inc., 1970. p. 273.

114 "The Bubble Has Burst." *The Louisiana Press-Journal* 27 Jul 1972.

115 "Town recalls 'Momo' saga." *Columbia Daily Tribune* 15 Jul 2012.

INDEX

P

R

S

T

Table Rock Lake, 103
Tazewell County, 43, 44, 155
Ted Shanks Conservation Area, 59
Tom Sawyer, 52, 53
Town Branch Creek, 82
track, 21, 22, 33, 41, 76, 119, 120, 121, 129, 143, 146

U

Unidentified Flying Object Bureau, 28
Upper Twin Mountain, 60

W

Wentzville, 41
Westmoreland County, 49, 50

Y

Yeti, 2, 3

Z

zoologist, 81

ABOUT THE AUTHOR

Amber DeVille

Lyle Blackburn is a full-time author, musician, and cryptid researcher from Texas. His investigative cryptozoology books reflect his life-long fascination with legendary creatures. Lyle has been heard on numerous radio programs, including *Coast To Coast AM*, and has been featured on television shows such as *Monsters and Mysteries in America*, *Finding Bigfoot*, and *Strange Evidence*. Lyle is also a writer for the monthly horror magazine, *Rue Morgue*, frontman for the rock band Ghoultown, and narrator of several Small Town Monsters documentary films, including *Boggy Creek Monster*, *The Mothman of Point Pleasant*, and *Bray Road Beast*.

When Lyle isn't writing books, chasing cryptids, or performing with his band, he can be found speaking at various cryptozoology conferences and horror conventions around the United States. Just look for the trademark black cowboy hat.

For more information, visit www.lyleblackburn.com

MORE BOOKS BY THE AUTHOR

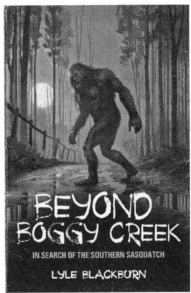

THE BEAST OF BOGGY CREEK:
THE TRUE STORY OF THE FOUKE MONSTER

The definitive book on the most infamous Southern mystery creature! The book covers the entire history of the Fouke Monster and the making of the horror film, *The Legend of Boggy Creek*. Includes a bonus sighting chronicle with details of over 70 visual encounters near Fouke, Arkansas. (Anomalist Books)

BEYOND BOGGY CREEK:
IN SEARCH OF THE SOUTHERN SASQUATCH

An in-depth exploration of the history and modern encounters with Bigfoot-like creatures across the southern United States. Join Lyle as he travels woods and waterways, delves into dusty archives, and interviews a host of credible eyewitnesses in search of fascinating legends, chilling accounts, and compelling evidence. (Anomalist Books)

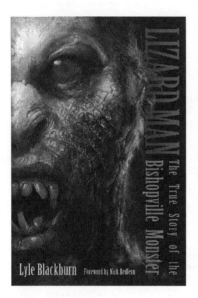 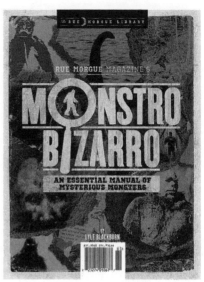

LIZARD MAN:
THE TRUE STORY OF THE BISHOPVILLE MONSTER

A fascinating and unprecedented look at one of the most bizarre and hair-raising cases of an unknown creature. Known locally as the "Lizard Man," the witnesses are convinced they've seen it, and the local law officials are backing them up. This is their story. (Anomalist Books)

MONSTRO BIZARRO:
AN ESSENTIAL MANUAL OF MYSTERIOUS MONSTERS

In the seventh installment from the Rue Morgue Library, legend hunter Lyle Blackburn explores the world of cryptozoology in cinema and culture (as he does in his Rue Morgue Magazine articles). The book features articles, photo galleries, cryptid files, and much more with a Foreword by director Eduardo Sanchez (*Exists*, *Blair Witch Project*) and contributions by Ken Gerhard, Nick Redfern, and David Weatherly. Full color with numerous photos and illustrations. (Rue Morgue Library)

38723088R00106

Made in the USA
Middletown, DE
10 March 2019